Who dropped the ball on our kids?

Who Dropped the Ball on Our Kids? The continuing miseducation of Black youth and its negative effective on their identity formation and economic power, first edition

Copyright © 2019 by Sondai K. Lester, P.S.E. Institute, Detroit, MI

ISBN number: 978-0-578-44944-9

Library of Congress Cataloguing-in-Publication Data

Lester, Sondai K.

Who Dropped the Ball on Our Kids? The continuing miseducation of Black youth and its negative effect on their identity formation and economic power

1. African American Education
2. African American History
3. Hidden Curriculum and African Americans

Editing by Lindiwe S. Lester; Cover design by Noni Lester Olayinka

Dedication

West African Adinkra symbol,

Nsoroma

(meaning: Their illumination is a reflection of God)

Dedicated to my children, Tarik and Noni, grandson Jide, and all Black children. I write with the hope that my generation's endeavors and those that follow will make a way for you to actualize the fullness of your treasured talents in this challenging world.

Acknowledgements

Oftentimes I wondered whether I was insane as thoughts ran through my mind about what appears to be a devastating impact of American education on Black people. I've been reassured by a number of people that I was neither insane nor alone in my observations. These ruminations about the American system of education have kept me awake at times, paranoid at others, and vacillating between hope and hopelessness in Black people's pursuit of change. Mostly, I've been inspired to keep the conversation going, trusting more will hear and heed in the interest of our shared yearning for freedom.

A number of faithful conversation partners over nearly 50 years bolster my belief that our thoughts and voices continue to matter. Among them, I acknowledge Kenneth Hill (founder of Detroit Area Pre-College Engineering Program [DAPCEP] and a similar initiative in Chicago), Ira K. Rutherford (retired school leader and superintendent), Dahia Shabaka (retired Detroit Public Schools' director of social studies, who was unrelenting in her insistence on African Centered Education), and my Kappa Alpha Psi brotherhood (with our monthly meetings that create a space for us to laugh, reminisce, and think together).

Much of who I have become is because of the nearly 30 years spent in ministry at the Shrine of the Black Madonna in Detroit and Atlanta and in comradeship with the members across the country. I am awed as I ponder my early and middle adult years at the Shrine. These years enabled a sharpening of my perspective on the nature of power, the systems that undergird it and how groups are impacted by that system based on their position, role and history.

I have been fortunate to engage with many dedicated educators and revolutionary thinkers, including the late Dr. Aombaye (Alvin) Ramsey. I hope these pages are in some way a celebration of his memory and vast contributions to the uplift of Black people. In recent years, I've found new fuel and a rekindling in the young activists and thinkers who are providing a contemporary lens on the issues of being Black in America. These inspiring voices include author Ta-Nehisi Coates, the Black Lives Matter movement and many more who challenge new generations to be "woke."

I'd also like to extend my sincerest gratitude to my good friend Dr. Diane Fabu Jackson for reading and contributing her candid, insightful analysis on this manuscript. Finally, I am infinitely appreciative of Lindiwe Stovall Lester, my wife and partner of more than 40 years, who supports, challenges and enhances my thinking and who patiently edits my writing.

Table of Contents

Who Dropped the Ball on our Kids? Sondai K. Lester

Introduction

"We in the United States live out our lives in a white-supremacist social order in which the economic, political and cultural interests of a European American elite dominate societal institutions—including what is taught in schools."
—Mw. J. Shujaa[1]

The following pages share a troubling, yet cautiously optimistic reflection on the Black educational experience and its relationship to the race-based power dynamics in the United States. This compilation of thoughts brings together key educational practices and more than 300 years of related scholarship that have and continue to impact social, economic and political outcomes for Black people. I've been razor-focused on examining this scholarship as it relates to its effect on the persistent efforts and varied strategies undertaken to liberate Black people from the harrowing effects of chattel slavery.

This book examines the history of ideas related to education that gave shape to the prevailing consciousness of both the white

---

[1] Shujaa, Mwalimu J., Editor, (1994). *Too Much School, Too Little Education: A Paradox of Black Life in White Societies*, p. 10

privilege group and oppressed groups—to this day. This entrenched consciousness assumes the "naturalness" of the system's arrangement, with the white group on top. And, for everyone else, being on the bottom is "just the way it's supposed to be."

I do not assume the educational system is a stand-alone institution in the enduring oppression of Black people. It, as one institution within the multi-webbed system, is complicit. Its practices, constructs and policies play a significant role in assuring the race-based maintenance of America's inequitable social and economic arrangement of groups.

This writing is personal. With 50 years in service to the liberation of Black people as both a teacher and leader, I am obligated to share what I've learned and witnessed hoping to contribute to the thinking and work of succeeding generations of leaders and teachers. While I am distressed about the current state of the Black condition, I am also heartened that new generations of thinkers and actors are equally committed to liberating Black minds and communities.

These pages are meant to be explicit in bringing to light the implicit, powerful agenda of schools. It's an agenda that has become so ingrained that most educators have little or no awareness that their "righteous" work of education is essentially a reinforcement and perpetuation of Black people's status as a second-class group.

I look forward to this rendering adding value to educators in rethinking *how* they educate Black children. Heightening parents' awareness of the covert role and effect of American schooling and aiding them in transforming schools is another aim. Parents can help ensure schools educate their children in ways that align with their aspirations for raising whole, confident, competent Black children. Alternative approaches to education must be sought so teaching and learning are carried out in a way that enables young people to see the world as it is and grasp who they are in that world. This includes developing them into astute observers of how that world impacts their self-identity. This approach to education can improve young people's efficacy in navigating and negotiating for success in the environment they are contending with today.

Any radical rearrangement of relationships between groups in this society requires a complete reassessment of the role of the school and how the school carries out that role. Schools must be more than a place to, at best, ready young people for employment in the jobs allocated for the poor and working class. It's imperative, if Black people are to rise from the pre-assigned lower and underclass stations in life, that our schools are places to not only perceive the world in terms of being a member of their racial group but determine how to change the arrangement of the group's position in it. Students, parents and educators must be acutely aware of how powerfully the curriculum shapes the nature

---

Those who control the school curriculum wield significant power over the minds of young people.

---

and quality of the students' thought processes. To move towards the educational quality for which the oppressed have yearned requires either reconstituting school curriculum or gaining adeptness at navigating it to extract only that which is beneficial to change the minds and status of the oppressed. Know this: *Those who control the school curriculum wield significant power over the minds of young people.*

Finally, the intent of this writing is to make clear for parents and educators that the work of education is not easy. There's much to overcome and strive towards. Extensive and relentless efforts have been undertaken over decades, even centuries, to build a body of ideas that promote white supremacy while deeply embedding an assumed, natural status of second-class citizenship for Black people. Educational, social and political outcomes, as such, with whites remaining squarely at the top and Blacks at the bottom, are not coincidental. They result from deliberate intent. The "miseducation" of Black people, as described by Carter G.

Woodson in 1933, has been unremitting and continues today with devastating effect.

The historical and current dismal socio-economic and other outcomes for Black people cannot be explained away as simply Blacks not trying hard enough. Even social scientists' findings, when attempting to explore root causes of these outcomes by attributing them to cyclical poverty, chronic poor housing, or crimes of depraved desperation, are insufficient. These are not root causes, but symptoms. Root cause rests within the historical, threaded pattern of a systematic, persistent institutional declaration (and ongoing reinforcing support) of white superiority and Black inferiority.

Even those who speak of outcomes as related to "post-traumatic slavery syndrome" are offering only a partial analysis. These insightful proponents of PTSS have probably not recognized the system of the past remains solidly in tact today. So, it's not only "post-traumatic" because widespread *present* trauma-inducing activity is ongoing. The web of American institutions not-so-clandestinely declares and reinforces an inferior nature and status for people of color as a way of life. So, here we are in the 21st century with systems, policies and practices that are part of a long history of continuous and contemporary reinforcement of status disparity between white and Black.

This book is organized in two sections. The first and main one lays out the history and impact of systemic racism in education. The second section offers suggestions to assist parents and educators in enabling Black children to attain quality education along with an affirming racial identity and solidarity.

As you read, know that you will not find a prescription to heal all that ails the educational system and the control it wields over the collective Black mind. This is more of a meditation; for some, hopefully, a stimulant. It is also a learning legacy of three friends in educational leadership for 50 years. It's a description with some considerations for educating today's Black children. By whatever name, these words are meant to help awaken minds and hearts, to reframe the thinking of everyone with a stake in the education, survival and thriving of Black children.

PART I: EDUCATION AND THE HISTORICAL, SYSTEMATIC OPPRESSION OF BLACK PEOPLE

Race and Education:
Yes, It's Personal

When a Black child enters the classroom, little does this young bright-eyed five-year-old know that the curriculum and all the educational constructs that shape learning are stacked against him. — Sondai Lester

Ira Rutherford, Kenny Hill, and I have a 50-year brotherhood—fused through our work and involvement in educating Black students as a vehicle for social change. Our bond had its infancy in the middle 1960s, a tumultuous period of activism, revolutionary thought and insistence on large-scale change for Blacks in white America. We were swept up in the vortex of revolutionary energy and have evolved over the 50 years. Yet we've remained focused on reforming education to empower and liberate Black students from the destructive psychological impact of the educational system.

Through the decades, we each channeled our efforts and poured our hearts into various organizations and initiatives intent on revolutionizing Black education. Alternately, we were in the classroom, leading community education initiatives, serving as school administrators, writing, developing supplemental educational programs, serving on boards to lead curriculum

Who Dropped the Ball on our Kids? Sondai K. Lester

reform, espousing liberation theology to make the church an instrument for transforming thinking, and more. Even now in 2018, when we gather monthly as 50-year fraternity brothers and friends, inevitably we will deliberate over what else we can do. Or we just reflect on the current state of Black people and the school systems. Occasionally, we ask ourselves: *Did we drop the ball? If so, when, why, where and how?*

Beginning in the 1960s, we developed a culturally-based analysis of the inadequacy of the educational process for Black young people. We believed, even before the phrase "hidden curriculum" emerged in scholarly literature, that public education had a hidden agenda grounded in the societal myth of white superiority and Black inferiority. In our analyses, bolstered by our experience in K-12 education, the purpose of public education was to serve as another powerful tool to compel both Black and white students to believe in these myths. This included developing and deepening attitudes and behaviors that supported and perpetuated the myths. This social conditioning has been unyielding in defining race relations in America.

What We Learned: Some Big Truths

The three of us, Kenny, Ira and I, shared and refined our understanding that the system of oppression (beginning with chattel slavery) and the subsequent laws and policies were justified through the myths of white supremacy and Black inferiority. By the middle of the 20th Century, this enduring physically and psychically-hostile racial environment had begun to morph (especially in the North). It became an *institutionalized* racism whereby the social systems generated policies that greatly restricted Black people's access to decent resources and opportunities. The schools were and are a part of this institutionalized racism. So, even though the American public education system implies that student achievement and outcomes are rooted in a meritocracy (i.e., based on individual accomplishments without bias), it, in fact, plays a role in ensuring Black people remained in an oppressed, marginalized, lower-class status. *Is it even possible for a Black child to be educated without bias in the current system?* She is raised in an environment that has declared her entire race biologically inferior and put in place structures with two sets of rules, one for whites and the other for Blacks.

These institutional structures are inescapable and meant to ensure darker people are securely situated at the bottom. Every American institution, with its policies, makes certain that Blacks remain in our designated place at the bottom. It doesn't matter whether it's media, education, law enforcement, courts, health, economics, regulatory, and the list goes on. Given that reality, it's implausible to think the Black student enters school on equal footing with white students or has much chance of "meriting" the same benefits that can accrue through quality education.

The "hidden curriculum" of the school has both a causative and additive effect. It ensures Black students have an internalized self-hatred and a pathological mindset that leads to an unwitting belief that white power and societal control are natural, reasonable, and inescapable. By uncritically and unconsciously accepting the white western worldview proffered by schools, all the key stakeholders—Black students, teachers and parents—buy into a value system that promotes selfish

> **Seemingly paradoxical, the process of education significantly limits the chance of a Black child developing his or her potential.**

personal interest and a continuing dream of assimilation into the white-controlled world. Seemingly paradoxical, the actual process of education significantly limits the chance of a Black child developing his or her potential.

Developing intellectually and psychologically would mean Black children would emerge from their schooling with two sets of skills. One provides the capacity to thrive in the world *and* the other affirms a positive sense of racial identification and urgency to own responsibility for the needs and power interests of the Black community. Controlled from within by the society's negative perception of Blackness, teachers have been blindly bound to and unable to disentangle from the "hidden curriculum." This means they haven't been much help in raising

Who Dropped the Ball on our Kids? Sondai K. Lester

the consciousness of Black children to see beyond the lies and distortions about everything that is Black—past or present.

What we learned: Big Truth #1

In any social system, its institutions provide the foundation and processes for human consciousness, expectations and behavior. In a system based on injustice, inequity, and the oppression of one group by another, that system's institutions propagate a historical perspective designed to rationalize and perpetuate those conditions. A primary role of those social institutions is to imbed in the minds of the oppressor and oppressed the "naturalness" and inescapability of each group's social status. That normalizing or sense of "naturalness" is grounded in the ideas that:

1. the system reflects a cosmic or divinely ordained human hierarchy,

2. one's biology (race) determines one's place in the hierarchy, and

3. resistance to one's placement in the hierarchy is unreasonable and an act of futility.

What we learned: Big Truth #2

Related to our Big Truth #1, the primary role of the school (along with the church, mass media and other institutions)

is to support the accepted social arrangement—delineated by race and class—by conditioning every student, both consciously and subconsciously, to know and take their place in the hierarchy. American institutions, both religious and secular, function as essential agents of socialization into a deeply engrained system of injustice and Black second-class status.

> **American institutions, both religious and secular, function as essential agents of socialization into a deeply engrained system of injustice towards Blacks.**

Bertrand Russell, late British philosopher and Nobel Prize winner, articulated this idea of the role of education in 1916:[2]

> *"Almost all education has a political motive: it aims at strengthening some group, national or religious or even social, in the competition with other groups. It is this motive, in the main, that determines the subjects taught, the knowledge offered, and the knowledge withheld, and decides what mental habits the pupils are expected to acquire. Hardly anything is done to foster inward growth of mind and spirit;* **in fact, those who have had the most education are very often atrophied in their mental and spiritual health."**

---

[2] From Education as a political institution, *The Atlantic*, June 1916

Who Dropped the Ball on our Kids? Sondai K. Lester

To view schools' content and curriculum solely as they relate to preparing individuals for meaningful employment is limiting. Failing to recognize their more crucial and powerful socialization function renders children of the oppressed nearly incapable of accurately assessing the reality of their world. Consequently, these young people and their parents are blind to their need to challenge the injustices doled out to them through their schooling. If parents expect their children to have a chance at achieving wholeness, there must be effort made to remove the blinders. It's well established that you can't do much about a problem without first becoming aware that it exists.

What we learned: Big Truth #3

Intertwined with Big Truths #1 and #2, we learned that schools do not exist in isolation from the larger structures and operations that perpetuate the inequities within society. *Schools are complicit,* a critical cog in the American networked system. The school exists foremost, through its "hidden curriculum," to lead all members of society to an unquestioned acceptance of the values and attendant behaviors that support the social status quo and its historical power relations. The content and curriculum of the schools emanate from an elaborate centuries-old process, which deliberately builds an ideological foundation to support white supremacy and Black inferiority.

Schools cannot be viewed separate from the larger institutional system and its intentions for all groups, based on race then class.

A "good" curriculum is still not enough

Even if, by a stroke of luck or through sheer ingenuity, the school has a "good" curriculum that fosters higher learning, it mistakenly assumes a Black child and a white child have come into school from the same world. It has not considered that America is "Two Nations[3]" —unequal and delineated based on race. So, even with the best intentions, the "good" curriculum is part of undermining the potential and healthy sense of self for the Black child.

With this keen awareness of the psychological damage done to Black students through the insidious curriculum, Kenny, Ira and I attempted to sprinkle seeds of change where we could—in the classrooms, hallways, school board meetings, administrative offices, after school programs and in parent groups. We focused on building or at least augmenting the educational experience of students to help undo the damage and psychic trauma of being Black in a whitewashed educational system. From the late1960s, we each exposed classroom students to writings by distinguished authors and researchers who challenged the validity of the white western worldview. We opened their minds to authors with seminal works that challenged 20th Century thinking. These

---

[3] Hacker, Andrew (1992), *Two Nations: Black and White, Separate, Hostile, Unequal*

Who Dropped the Ball on our Kids? Sondai K. Lester

included but were not limited to: Lerone Bennett (Before the Mayflower), John Henrik Clarke (Marcus Garvey and the Vision of), Ivan Van Sertima (They Came Before Columbus), Alex Haley (Autobiography of Malcolm X), Maya Angelou (I Know Why the Caged Bird Sings), Richard Wright (Black Boy), James Baldwin (The Fire Next Time), and Ralph Ellison (Invisible Man).

We were deliberate in our efforts to build cohorts of educated Black youth at each of the institutions where we were assigned. It was refreshing that many of these youth were psychologically and intellectually ready to reject much of the negative conditioning of the larger white society. One experience, emblematic of the eagerness with which students yearned to "know" themselves, their histories, and their stories comes to mind from the mid-1960s. When I decided to distribute Lerone Bennett's Before the Mayflower as a substitute for the standard middle school U. S. history text, it seemed a fire was ignited among the students. It triggered another fire as well, since this was long before Black studies or African Centered Education was a sanctioned approach to framing social studies. I was reprimanded (and almost fired) by the principal and assistant principal for this alleged act of defiance. When I refused to conform to their mandate to get back to the prescribed curriculum, I was sent to the regional superintendent for a disciplinary conference. Somehow, my students got word of what had occurred and learned of the possibility that I could be removed from the school. When I returned, they were outside of

Who Dropped the Ball on our Kids? Sondai K. Lester

the school protesting, demanding that I remain their teacher. The issue was dropped; and I continued exposing them to their own history (although I never gained any love from the principal).

Following the students' exposure to Bennett's <u>Before the Mayflower</u>, I began bringing in more books from Black bookstores. Detroit's Vaughn's Bookstore became a frequent spot for securing these books. That led to hosting Black book sales for the students. Imagine throngs of students from economically poor neighborhoods lined up around the walls and halls to buy these books. They were there—hungry for self-knowledge, to experience their history, heroes and heroines, struggles, and centuries of grand accomplishments.

When students entered our classrooms, we made sure they were walking into a safe, powerful, and racially affirming place that stood in contrast to the negative symbols all around them of what it meant to be Black in America.

When students entered our classrooms, we made sure they were walking into a safe, powerful, and racially affirming place that stood in contrast to the negative symbols of what it meant to be Black in America. We immersed them in both written and visual symbols that reflected a very different racial image than what they saw on television and the disparate quality of life in

Black and white communities. They were exposed to imagery of powerful Black leaders (such as Angela Davis, Huey Newton and Bobby Seale). They heard poetic utterances (Don Lee and Nikki Giovanni, for example) that loudly proclaimed: "We are more than good enough. We are kings and queens!" I am convinced this was one of the few periods during which Black students enjoyed social studies. But why would they enjoy a subject that is typically totally devoid of any positive representation of who the students taking the course were? The topics in social studies classes (generally lacking any relationship to their current reality) would hardly inspire student interest.

Was cultural learning just a fad?

During the latter part of the 20th Century, school leaders began to move away from the social-cultural perspective which was at the core of our thinking about and engagement in teaching and learning. This perspective had been foundational to our view that education ought to have some grounding in addressing each student's "inner reality" as well as focus on how the external world impacts that inner state. We had spent considerable energy building on the writings of Black intellectuals promoting an African-Centered approach to educating Black children. That approach began losing ground by the late 1990s.

The social-cultural lens on education was displaced by a concentration on the external world. There was increased

Who Dropped the Ball on our Kids? Sondai K. Lester

emphasis on content mastery (especially in math and science) and standardized test scores. Yet, here we are closing out the second decade of the 21st Century, and even with the keen focus on content mastery, American educational achievement (a common predictor of life success) remains subpar. This is especially true when compared to other first-world countries, and it's *dismally* low among lower income students and racial minorities.

As improved social status and higher income became associated with careers in math and science, the primary goal of schools shifted to preparing students to qualify for the emerging technology jobs. Consequently, an increasing amount of the curricular resources were directed towards staff development and courses in those areas. Systematic, in-depth social-cultural inquiry lost its place in public school curriculum. It began to be seen as inconsequential, if not completely irrelevant among educators and parents. It's not surprising then that social studies in Black school districts began rapidly receding into the background, losing the vitality previously gained through a focus on African studies and African Centered Education. This occurred in tandem with the practice of allocating decreasing resources to develop teachers to effectively and creatively teach social science courses.

This curricular shift away from social science created a dichotomy between schooling as the means to earn high incomes (through science and math fields) and providing an education that develops young people into critically-thinking and socially-responsible individuals. The latter is represented by social science studies. A significant income inequality exists between careers in science, technology, engineering and math (STEM) and those in the social sciences (where human personality, human behavior and social realities are influenced most). This wage disparity became a disincentive—diminishing aspiring teachers' interest in pursuing social science careers.

The collective body of educators (including the three of us), through curriculum mandate, began to primarily emphasize math and science content mastery. We unwittingly relinquished our roles as the watchdogs and champions of the social-cultural lens on schooling that defines and shapes human identity. Lacking the social-cultural perspective and voice, the Detroit Public Schools, for example, succumbed to the new curricular themes, abandoning the African Centered curricular foundation in the early 2000s. It had been less than a decade since African Centered Education had been *demanded* by many in the Black community, then formally adopted.

Kenny, Ira and I along with a cadre of conscious educators witnessed the public-school system devolving into a different educational perspective. This version declares there is a singular, objective social studies relevant for all students regardless of class or racial grouping. This was an impetus for the public-school system to promote the flawed notion that we live in a "post-racial" society where equal opportunity and meritocracy rule.

The view that the inner world of the child is less important than the external needs of the marketplace became the norm for schooling as we entered the 21st Century. Activist-educators' voices diminished. This happened either through the retirement of school teachers and administrators or through the sheer weight of the system to rid itself of any semblance of an African Centered approach to teaching and learning.

Now, in retrospect, we ask ourselves after 50 years of striving to make education matter for Black people: *Did we drop the ball? If not, who dropped it? If so, where do we go now?*

Why the shift away from Black culture matters

The waning, if not total abandonment, of a radical social-cultural context for educating Black students along with the failure to restructure the curriculum to meet the employability needs of the modern world, undoubtedly has a role in the rapid fragmentation of the Black community. Eliminating this critical context through which Black young people could make meaning of the changes and disruptions in society is damaging beyond belief. The loss of an African Centered curriculum along with the seeming collapse of hope of being accepted as equals in the white world (through the dream of integration) further undermined Black people's "tribal" or fraternal connection. Predictably, these diminished feelings of social responsibility to create and maintain our communities soon followed. Simultaneously, the Black revolutionary consciousness so prominent in the 1960s, 70s and 80s faded or splintered; among other causes, they lacked effective organizing strategies for fighting for liberation in the new global, technological context.

With this loss of connection and obligation to one another, it's easier to violate intra-racial behavioral boundaries that were formerly viewed as part and parcel of our shared sacred bonds. Too many in the Black community, without blinking, violently prey upon each other; even the old and the very young are victimized to serve narrow self-interests. This socially destructive behavior is a by-product of Black "miseducation." Indeed, there is something to be said about removing African and Black historical and cultural studies from the school curriculum. Wouldn't the absence of any learning that gives a positive grounding to Black youth influence their psychology and actions, their norms and boundaries? **When nothing in their learning helps create or enhance connective tissue with their own community, it's not a stretch that this lack could have a devastating, lasting effect.**

To follow is an examination of the history of the educational system, its variations over time, and how it consistently kept systemic racism alive. The schools, part of an institutional network, worked in hand-in-hand with all the other American institutions whose interactions with Blacks were shaped by the same pernicious "white superior-Black inferior" worldview.

American public education's history of systemic racism

"It would be extremely naïve to expect the dominant classes to develop a type of education that would enable subordinate classes to perceive social injustices critically." - Paulo Freire[4]

The Foundations of Modern American Education

The December 10, 2006 issue of <u>Time Magazine</u> included a feature article titled *How to Bring Our Schools Out of the 20th Century*. The basic premise of the piece was that today's school curriculum is outdated, a relic of a 20th Century existence that is dead and gone—displaced by new modes of thinking and acting. These 20th Century curricula still used by schools are preparing students for skills incompatible with the needs of the 21st Century, post-industrial global economy. Without question, we know there are implications for America's white students. However, for Blacks (and others relegated to second-class status), these adverse consequences are exacerbated.

---

[4] Paulo Freire (1985). *The Politics of Education: Culture, Power, and Liberation*, South Hadley, MA, Bergin & Garvey

Clash of eras: Industrial and technological

The curriculum and organization of most of today's schools are based on educational concepts developed in the late 19th Century in response to the needs of the emerging industrial era. As manufacturing began to supplant the market demands and jobs of the agricultural age, this shift required developing an educational system compatible with those changes.

Industrialism led to the mechanization of products using mass production machinery. Factories proliferated as they became the economic centers for mass-production of consumer goods. The labor-intensive farm work also began to increasingly be performed by machines fabricated in these factories. Industrialism meant job growth took place mostly in factories, while job shrinkage occurred on farms. Out of work farm laborers began flocking into the cities (largely the North and Midwest) to take advantage of these jobs being created in the factories. Along with the movement of farm laborers out of the South to the northern industrial core came the influx of two other sizeable groups: 1) European immigrants (escaping poverty and economic turmoil) and 2) African Americans (fleeing the brutal Jim Crow South).

Migration data indicate between 1880 and 1920, 20 million Europeans immigrated to the United States settling primarily on the east coast and in the Midwest. Between 1916 and 1970, six million Blacks migrated out of the rural south to the urban

Who Dropped the Ball on our Kids? Sondai K. Lester

northeast, Midwest, and western United States—known as "The Great Migration."

Industrialization affected more than jobs. During the agricultural era, farming consumed most of the time and energy of the entire family. Children, if they attended school at all, did so only during the farming off-season. A child's life was centered around and controlled by the rigors and demands of planting and harvesting on their family's land or toiling (along with the rest of the family) on an affluent white farmer's land. In this farming culture, children were typically in continuous contact with their parents, most often side-by-side engaged in the grueling farm activities from sun-up to sundown. The family lived together near the area where the farm work was performed. As such, children spent little time apart from their parents.

That dynamic (of children being in close contact with their parents most of the time) shifted with the industrial age. This social shift into what Toffler called The Second Wave is described in his book, The Third Wave[5]:

> "...the Second Wave concentrated more than energy. It also concentrated population, stripping the countryside of people and relocating them in giant urban centers. It even concentrated work. While work in the First Wave societies took place everywhere—in

---

[5] Toffler, Alvin (1980). *The Third Wave.* Bantam Books.

Who Dropped the Ball on our Kids? Sondai K. Lester

the home, in the village, in the fields—much of the work in the Second Wave societies was done in factories where thousands of laborers were together under a single roof." p. 69

The daily labor of individual adults, rather than the farming family, was the foundation of the industrial era. Most of these predominantly male workers, for the first time, labored alongside other men with whom they had no familial relationships. In contrast to farm production, which was based on the family's collective efforts, industrial age factory work was dependent on the individual efforts of men separate from their families. In this

---

A new question arose out of this new industrial age lifestyle: *What should be done with the children while the parents are away at work?*

---

new work configuration, they were producing goods they neither needed for their daily lives nor could afford.

Urbanization's economic impact further affected the social arrangement of families; the cost of living was significantly higher in urban cities than in the rural agricultural South. This frequently required mothers to leave the home and their children to take on menial jobs. A new question arose out of this emerging industrial age lifestyle: *What should be done with the children while the parents are away at work?* Attention was then shifted to reshaping the role of

Who Dropped the Ball on our Kids? Sondai K. Lester

schools in light of the growing number of children at home unattended during parents' work hours.

As the industrial age unfolded, the movement for compulsory government-funded public education simultaneously gained steam. As early as the middle of the 19th Century, states had begun passing legislation mandating 1) students attend school up to a certain age and 2) the government fund those schools. Horace Mann, the secretary of education for Massachusetts between 1837 and 1848, was the driving force behind the **compulsory education movement.** Mann worked to create a statewide system of public schools based on the Prussian model, which used age-assigned grades and lecture as the fundamental teaching strategy. Soon, other states, particularly in the North, began setting up their own public-school systems. By the close of the 19th Century, free public education was available to all U.S. children. Black children were educated to a lesser degree and quality in this post-chattel slavery period but theoretically public education was open to all. Black children attended segregated, underfunded schools and were forced to use second-hand textbooks.

Beginning with Massachusetts in 1852, all states had passed compulsory attendance laws by 1918, which required completion of elementary school. By then, half of the children attending school were educated in one-room schools. At that time, there

Who Dropped the Ball on our Kids? Sondai K. Lester

was a very different view of secondary education (high school) than is common today. For one, attending high school was not yet legally mandatory. It had been conceived with a sense of exclusivity—as preparatory academies for college. In the 19th Century landscape, these were institutions for the societal elite, children of the white wealthy privileged class. In 1890, only seven percent of high school aged children were enrolled. The number of 14 to 17-year olds enrolled in high school began to quickly rise during the 20th Century, in conjunction with industrialization. There were two million high school students by 1920, up from one million in 1910 and 200,000 in 1890.[6]

The industrial age's fundamental question concerning what to do with children while their parents worked away from the home, was being answered by the expansion of the public-school system. The compulsory attendance laws, which increased the number of 14 to 17 year olds attending high school, helped alleviate the

> By the early 20th century, responsibility for, and more importantly, control and socialization of children shifted away from the home to the school.

[6] Mirel, Jeff and Angus, David. High Standards for All? The Struggle for Equality in the American High School Curriculum, 1890-1990. *American Educator*, Summer 1994.

Who Dropped the Ball on our Kids? Sondai K. Lester

problem. Responsibility for, and more importantly, control and socialization of children shifted away from the home to the school. The school teacher was gradually becoming a surrogate parent and child care worker during the parents' working hours.

As the school became a central aspect of society and family life, it became a priority for educators to take an in-depth look at the kind of curriculum that would be compatible with the needs and dynamics of this new industrial economy. Another critical question arose: *How does this early 20th Century new industrial age impact the knowledge and skills required for success in this economy?*

White think tank's solution for industrial age education

On one level industrialism could absorb the semi-literate, unskilled masses of people migrating to the cities. They were hired into factories and performed dock work where manufactured goods would be produced and shipped across the world. Jobs in steel mills, foundries, and auto plants were primarily based on muscle power, requiring little mental effort.

On another level, these factories created the need for an expanding managerial class capable of comprehending management systems and technical processes to efficiently operate the new work structures. This managerial class required a higher level of knowledge and skills than the factories' muscle-driven worker bees. Their educational emphasis was on mental

Who Dropped the Ball on our Kids? Sondai K. Lester

rather than physical capability. These managerial workers were required to read, comprehend and apply new management theory.

Recognition that industrial era businesses needed people with literacy and language skills beyond what was typical of the agricultural era or what could be achieved just through elementary education led to a heightened focus on secondary education. In contrast to the 19th Century high school as an elite college preparatory institution, compulsory education laws of the early 20th Century were extended. They would begin to include high school for all, at least up until the age of 16. Developing a skilled managerial class was critical for the new factory-based economic engine and was one force behind the new high school participation laws. This was alongside the high school's new role of providing a place for young people to be housed and cared for while their parents worked in factories. Consider: In 1900 about six percent of American teenagers graduated from high school; by 1996 that number reached 85%.[7]

As the public high school rose in importance during the industrial era, educators began redefining the appropriate purpose and structure for secondary education. In the 1890s, the National Education Association (NEA) organized the Committee of Ten to deal with the issue. The Committee was made up of college

---

[7] Mirel, Jeffrey and Angus, David. High Standards for All? The Struggle for Equality in the American High School Curriculum, 1890-1990. *American Educator*, Summer 1994.

presidents and deans of the leading prep schools and was chaired by Charles Eliot, the President of Harvard University.[8]

The Committee, whose purpose was to bring structure and consistency to the high school curriculum, concluded that all high school students should pursue a college preparatory curriculum. Eliot, as noted by Mirel, declared:

> *"Every subject which is taught in high school should be taught in the same way and to the same extent to every pupil so long as he pursues it, no matter what the probable destination of the student may be, or at what point his education is to cease."*

The Committee of Ten's egalitarian approach to education meant provision of a rigorous liberal arts education to all students. It would feature programs specializing in classical languages, science, mathematics, literature and specific electives.

Rise of unequal education: Race, class, testing and tracking

In light of the significant shift in the makeup of the population (with the increasing number of European immigrants and Blacks migrating to the industrialized North), the white power elite faced a critical challenge. *In the face of expanded educational requirements, how do we control these new citizenry groups so they do not become a threat to the*

---

[8] Mirel, Jeffrey, The traditional high school, *Education Next*, Vol. 6:1, 2006

white elites' economic power in this transition from an agricultural to industrial-based system?

It became clear that with the growing need to expand educational access to the masses, schooling had to be structured in a way that preserved the status quo. How would the burgeoning student population be educated to accept the logic and naturalness of the existing power arrangement in America? How would education discourage any inclination towards radicalism and social change? Answering these questions would be the focus of both politicians and educators throughout the 20th Century. These were not concerns of the Committee of Ten as they made efforts to define the content of the high school curriculum; others however were concerned and made plans to address them.

One response to these queries was the formation of another group within the NEA in 1918. This group called itself the Commission on the Reorganization of Secondary Education. This new caucus rejected the egalitarian position of the Committee of Ten, supporting instead the writings of renowned psychologist G. Stanley Hall. According to Mirel, Hall believed "most high school students were part of a great army of incapables who should be in schools for dullards or subnormal children."[9] Soon, other educators began to break from the Committee of Ten's view that

---

[9] Ibid.

Who Dropped the Ball on our Kids? Sondai K. Lester

all youth were to be provided an equal education and instead coalesced around Hall's thinking.

The Commission on the Reorganization of Secondary Education, unlike the Committee of Ten, was made up of representatives from colleges of education and high school educators. They called for *differentiated* programs to serve the new, diverse high school population. In its final report, *Cardinal Principles of Secondary Education*, the commission laid out two assumptions underlying their call for differentiated programs:

1. Most high school students were less intelligent than previous generations.
2. Since these new students lacked the intellectual ability, aspirations, and financial means to attend college, it was useless to demand they follow a college prep program.

The Commission declared that the source of educational inequality across class and race was the failure to allow for academic differentiation, which would allow students to follow their own interests, abilities and needs.

These two assumptions of the Cardinal Principles formed the foundation of educational thinking during the early 20th Century. The *comprehensive high school* was the product of these two principles. Supporters of the comprehensive high school defined equal education as equal access for all students to various academic programs based on interest and ability. The comprehensive high school was highly influenced by intelligence tests that were being developed during this same period. Subsequent to that, was the tracking of students based on these test scores. These practices allowed guidance counselors to assign students to the curriculum they thought suitable for their so-called objectively measured level of intelligence. With the new comprehensive high school, Mirel says: "America entered an era of democratic dumbing down; the equal opportunity to choose for oneself (or be chosen for) failing programs."[10]

> ...with the development of the comprehensive high school: "America entered an era of democratic dumbing down; the equal opportunity to choose for oneself (or be chosen for) failing programs."

The comprehensive high school allowed the public education system to funnel students into different educational programs of varying rigor, discipline, standards, and life possibilities, then award them all the same diploma. It's no wonder so many urban students can leave school with limited basic skills. Is anyone shocked that if educators enter the classroom with low expectations that low accomplishment will be the result?

---

[10] Mirel, Jeffrey, The traditional high school, *Education Next*, Vol. 6:1, 2006

Who Dropped the Ball on our Kids? Sondai K. Lester

The collapse of the national economy during the Great Depression, and with it the youth labor market, caused the high school student population to increase by a dramatic 73%. That is, between 1930 and 1960, the high school population rose to over seven million. This striking enrollment increase (with many of the students from lower-income families and racial minorities) led to a strengthening of the position that the new entrants had lower intellectual and academic abilities. The same was believed about the mass of European immigrants flooding to America during this period. School leaders were convinced that these "less-capable" students required less rigorous courses. Subsequently, the comprehensive high school with its tracking system increasingly assigned greater numbers of students to a non-academic general education curriculum (based to a great extent on race and economic status, i.e., Blacks, European immigrants' children and poor whites). This less-rigorous, lower learning tracking virtually ensured these students were relegated to the margins of the economy, qualified for only the lowest-paying, dead-end jobs.

> This less-rigorous, lower learning tracking virtually ensured these students were relegated to the margins of the economy, qualified for only the lowest-paying, dead-end job.

A personal example of this tracking and assigning was shared with me by a close friend, who, in the late 1960s, attended an inner-city junior high school and tested three grade levels above the norm in reading, comprehension and mathematics on the standardized test (then called the Iowa tests). Her "brilliance" was lauded by her counselors who worked with the neighboring *comprehensive* high school to have her moved from the eighth grade to the 11th grade. Her father challenged this idea as ridiculous given she had not yet taken higher level math and science courses. One educator remarked, "She can take general math and be just fine as an 11th grader." Fortunately, her father declined the offer and recognized their naïve, yet damaging plan would undermine her development. (All involved were Black educators, so he assumed it was not a deliberate conspiracy). They saw no issue with fast-tracking her to a comprehensive, general studies high school. Certainly, she was not the only student in the school with advanced academic ability who suffered intellectually because the school did not offer a rigorous, challenging educational experience.

The comprehensive high school with its differentiated curriculums and tracking system, which focused on the poor and non-white students, brought an insidious, destructive anti-intellectualism into the educational process for schools populated by those students. This anti-intellectualism led to a slow decline in the number of students matriculating in higher-order thinking, academic classes. Consequently, a significant number of students were leaving high school unprepared to succeed then, even now.

As a part of the early 20th Century school movement, members of the Commission on the Reorganization of Secondary Education and its Cardinal Principles were key to ingraining public school education with the notion that non-American white immigrant groups and Blacks are intellectually inferior. The development of the comprehensive high school was a product of that belief. Whether by conscious design or an unconscious adaptation, the society's racial and class bias within school systems became an instrument for the maintenance and preservation of the unequal, discriminatory distribution of wealth and power. This bias ensured the educational processes kept Blacks at the bottom.

Maintaining white economic control required new approaches to social control; this led to school reform. It must not be forgotten that prior to industrialism, education was mostly the domain of the white elite. Wealth exploded through the utilization of new urban laborers; thus, vigorous school reform took place to ensure new school structures were put in place to support the maintenance and control of this new workforce.

On one level, school reform needed to address the low-wage industrial workers in general and their acceptance of the existing economic hierarchy. On another level, the issue related to Blacks specifically, who were still seen as inferior to all whites regardless of economic class. So, schools needed to be a part of keeping Blacks on an even lower level than the poor working-class whites.

So as a *conserving* institution, the reformed schools set out to conserve and fulfill the the following social control functions (to be explored further in the next section).

Don't forget these social control functions of schools:

- ✓ Sustain the concentrations of wealth and power among the few white elite
- ✓ Diminish the desire to rebel on the part of the Black oppressed
- ✓ Ensure the sense that lower-class whites are secure in their superiority over Blacks, on the basis of their membership in the white race
- ✓ Make provision for laborers to acquire just enough knowledge to keep them capable of performing the jobs that create tremendous wealth for the white top level elites

Education's Social Control Function

"The school curriculum is not neutral knowledge. Rather, what counts as legitimate knowledge is the result of complex power relations, struggles, and compromises among identifiable class, race, and religious groups." Michael Apple, The Text and Cultural Politics, 1992.

T he schools serve as a primary instrument of social control, with an impact that has far-reaching, adverse implications for Black people. Social control includes determining and limiting one's range of "acceptable" behaviors and attitudes. The social control function of schools is precisely why groups tend to settle into the life stations where they find themselves. It is all by design, permeating the function of schools and the web of other institutions.

This notion of the school as primarily an instrument of social control, placement and a vehicle for the preservation of the status quo is further elaborated in Giroux and Penna's discourse on the "hidden curriculum."[11]

The school, at its core, is a conserving, not transforming, institution.

[11] Giroux, Henry and Penna, Anthony. Social Education in the Classroom: The Dynamics of the Hidden Curriculum. *Theory and Research in Social Education*, V11:1, Spring 1979

The authors put forth the idea that students, with few exceptions, are being unconsciously prepared to take the place in society prescribed and validated for them through the school's *hidden curriculum*. The purpose and function of schools goes beyond its general offering of courses and curricular choices. The failure of public education to alter the societal structures of power and place is, in part, the result of educators failing to grasp the relationship between school knowledge and the maintenance of the status quo. The school, at its core, is a conserving, not transforming, institution.

The on-going effort to reform and improve schools, especially as it relates to the education of racial minorities and the poor, has focused mostly on the objective dimensions of schooling: *Number of hours in the school day. Number of days in the school year. After school activities. Teacher preparation. Classroom size. Utilization of technology and so on.* Only a scant number of educators explore the interconnection between social ideology, instruction and curriculum. According to Michael Apple in *The Text and Cultural Politics*, educators need to:

> *"examine critically not just how a student acquires knowledge (the dominant question in the field of educational research) but why and how particular aspects of the collective culture are presented in the school as objective, factual knowledge. How concretely may official knowledge represent ideological configurations of the dominant*

interests in a society? How do schools legitimate these limited and partial standards of knowing as unquestioned truths?" [12]

This focus by most educators on the tangible, objective processes of education has failed to close the achievement gap—clearly delineated by race and class. Nor has overcoming the dismal educational outcomes for those demographic groups gotten any real traction. The achievement gap between Black and white students has remained static during the last 50 years despite the so-called efforts towards progress and parity during this last half century (Camera, 2016).[13] Hanushek, a Stanford University Hoover Institute senior fellow, in analyzing the update of the 1965 Coleman Report which had the deliberate intent of closing the white-black education achievement gaps, reported in 2016:

> *"After nearly a century of supposed progress in race relations within the United States, the modest improvement in achievement since 1965 can only be called a 'national embarrassment.' Put differently, if we continue to close gaps at the same rate in the future, it will be roughly two and a half centuries before the black-white math gap closes and one and a half century until the reading gap closes."* [14]

---

[12] Apple, Michael. The text and cultural politics. *Educational Researcher*, 1992. V: 21:7, p. 4-19

[13] Camera, Lauren, Achievement gap between white and black still gaping. *US News and World Report*, January 13, 2016.

[14] Hanushek, Eric A., What matters for student achievement. *Education Next*, Spring 2016, V16:2.

Who Dropped the Ball on our Kids? Sondai K. Lester

Why is this the case? Why have all the sincere efforts directed at reform that improves educational outcomes fallen so dismally short? These and other efforts have fallen flat and will continue to do so because the reformers haven't critically analyzed the socio-cultural foundations and purpose of education. They've either ignored or are blind to the fact that schools are conserving, not transforming, institutions. That being true, what then are they seeking to conserve? White superiority and primacy and Black inferiority and second-class status; these are, at least, covertly fundamental and non-negotiables. At best, reformers have naively assumed that the ideology undergirding the general curriculum is based on a truthful and accurate assessment of past and present socio-economic realities in America.

When the school is detached from any awareness of the socio-cultural foundation of education, reformers ought not expect to bring about any real change in minority student outcomes and racial disparities. Reform carried out within the context of an acceptance of the dominant socio-cultural perspective serves only to perpetuate the status quo. Perhaps that is their intent, whether reformers admit it or not.

How must individuals, who are serious about educational effectiveness that accomplishes or is directed at enabling Black people to transcend second-class oppressed status, approach that

Who Dropped the Ball on our Kids? Sondai K. Lester

process? To be effective, **educational reform must be undertaken based on:**

> 1) a systematic analysis of the way the *macro* or larger external economic and cultural forces influence the *micro* internal forces, i.e., those operating within an individual school, and

> 2) answering the question of how the basic ideology of the larger system, including the socio-economic organization of society influences the curriculum and interaction of students with teachers, each other, the educational process and the larger community outside of the school.

Schools are socio-political institutions charged with the socialization of its constituents. The aim is for them to accept and adapt to the ideas and interests of the dominant group in America. Schools prepare students to "fit in"—to willingly take their specific slot in the caste system, which undergirds and sustains the superior power position of the white dominant group at the expense of all others. That means **schools are counter-revolutionary entities.** School processes weaken if not totally incapacitate the desire and urgency of those consigned

> **Schools prepare students to "fit in"—to willingly take their specific slot in the caste system that undergirds and sustains the power and superior positions of the dominant group**

to the lower rungs of society to rise, strategize and resist their institutionally-reinforced inferior status.

The late Ralph Tyler, a well-respected educational analyst and researcher of the middle 20th Century, states that every educational philosophy emerges out of one of two conflicting positions:[15]

1. Should the schools develop young people to fit into the present society as it is? Or
2. Does the school have a revolutionary mission to develop young people who will seek to transform and improve society?

Paulo Freire, the Brazilian educator, reached similar conclusions to Tyler's regarding the two possible roles of schools. Freire says:

> *"There is no such thing as a neutral educational process. Education either functions as an instrument which is used to facilitate the integration of the younger generation into the logic of the present system and bring about conformity to it. Or it becomes the practice of freedom— the means by which men and women deal critically with reality and discover how to participate in the transformation of their world."*[16]

---

[15] Tyler, Ralph, *Basic Principles of Curriculum and Instruction*, University of Chicago Press, 1949
[16] Paulo Freire (2014). *Pedagogy of the Oppressed: 30th Anniversary Edition*, p.34, Bloomsbury Publishing USA

Who Dropped the Ball on our Kids? Sondai K. Lester

Our suspicions confirmed: There's a "Hidden Curriculum"

How exactly do schools, as agents of socialization, prime and prepare students to accept their assigned "place" in a society based on racism, economic inequality, and exploitation? Schools have two curriculums. One is the formal or "mainstream" curriculum which is explicitly outlined in documents prepared by the school for teachers, students, parents and the general community. These documents sketch out the framework for education including features such as school mission, grade-specific content for each academic discipline, requirements to advance from grade to grade, assessment schedules, and extra-curricular options.

The second curriculum is the "hidden curriculum," which is deeply rooted in the message systems and symbols of the schooling process. This includes such elements as: the curriculum itself (what is and is not included), pedagogical styles, systems of evaluation, and how students are organized and assigned to classes. Alongside the formal, overt curriculum with its mission statement and subject area content, the covert curriculum shrewdly transmits tacit messages related to acceptable attitudes, beliefs, values, behaviors and social place. Examples

> The "hidden curriculum" is deeply embedded in the message systems and symbols of the schooling process.

Who Dropped the Ball on our Kids? Sondai K. Lester

abound, and the Christopher Columbus legend is but one, although a good one: *Did Columbus really discover America? Were there indigenous people with established cultures already in the Americas when he arrived? Who were they? What happened to them?* Not only that, even with the fallacy of his discovery now unraveled, 500 years later children are still taught this inglorious lie and believe Columbus to be a hero worth celebrating.

The suspicion Kenny, Ira and I held about the hidden agenda of schools was extensively explored by educational scholars and critics. Paulo Freire (beginning with <u>Pedagogy of the Oppressed</u>), bell hooks (<u>Teaching to Transgress: Education as a Practice of Freedom,</u> 1994), Jonothan Kozol (<u>Savage Inequalities</u>) and Jean

> **The purpose of the hidden curriculum is cultural transmission of a specific worldview and social control.**

Anyon (<u>Social Class and the Hidden Curriculum of Work</u>) are but a handful of the theorists who explored the reality and negative effects of a hidden curriculum.

The purpose of the hidden curriculum is cultural transmission of a specific worldview and social control. It serves to maintain the status quo, specifically the preservation of control by the dominant economic elite within society by making provision for:

- **A continual flow of subservient workers**

- An acceptance of the existing hierarchy of social power and control

- A legitimizing of inequality

- A myth of meritocracy (you only have yourself and your inadequacy to blame if you are not successful)

- A justification of privilege for the few over the majority

Unlike what we are taught to believe, the public education system does not support the development of healthy skepticism, inquisitiveness, or curiosity among students when it comes to the logic and legitimacy of the inequality within society. Rather than cultivating an expansive mind, Black schools with the hidden curriculum limit and impede thinking. It's no wonder there's little revolt against the systemic racism in America.

> **Rather than cultivating an expansive mind, Black schools through the hidden curriculum limit and impede thinking.**

The public educational system conforms to Ralph Tyler's first philosophical option: *fitting students into the world as it exists— conditioning them to adapt to the status quo.* Says Michael Apple:

> "*There is little doubt that **the public schools are a choice transmission belt for the traditional rather than the***

innovative, much less what is radical. As a result, they facilitate the political socialization of the mainstream young and tend to equip them with the tools necessary for the particular roles they are expected to play in a given society, roles that for the most part do not serve their common interests."[17]

Jean Anyon (*Social Class and the Hidden Curriculum of Work*[18]) extensively investigated the function of the hidden curriculum. She studied it through the lens of class (not racial) implications. She discovered that public schools design varying types of educational experiences depending on the student's social class and the slots within society pre-established for them. The schools reinforce beliefs, values, and behaviors befitting the social class of most of the student attendees; they deliver what is required for them to effectively fulfill the roles assigned to their social class.

Anyon's studies revealed that the hidden curriculum for *working class* schools was directed at or molded students who:

1. easily adjusted to the mindless repetitive class room work requiring little analytical thought,

2. learned to be blindly obedient to authority, and

---

[17] Apple, Michael. The text and cultural politics. *Educational Researcher*, 1992, V: 21:7, p. 4-19

[18] Anyon, Jean. Social class and the hidden curriculum of work. *Journal of Education*, 1980, 162: 1, pgs. 67-92.

Who Dropped the Ball on our Kids? Sondai K. Lester

3. accepted, as permanent and irrevocable, the societal status quo with its unequal distribution of wealth and power.

Those schools put the greatest emphasis on students following instructions as outlined by the teacher. Attempts at independent thinking were viewed as acts of disobedience and unacceptable disruptions in the classroom. It was taboo for students to question the soundness of ideas, nor were they given the opportunity to choose other ways to approach the problems presented to them. Says Anyon:

> *"Work in these schools is often evaluated, not according to whether it is right or wrong but if the children followed the right directions given by the teacher.*[19]*"*

Teachers tended to be more amenable to giving higher grades to students who demonstrate the "right" behaviors and answers over those who might be equally or more proficient but who challenge the acceptable ways of viewing the subject matter. Choicelessness, obedience and acquiescence to the hierarchy are

Choicelessness, obedience and acquiescence to the hierarchy are the implicit curricular themes for the working-class schools.

---

[19] Ibid. Anyon. J.

Who Dropped the Ball on our Kids? Sondai K. Lester

the implicit curricular themes in schools for the working-class.

It's not uncommon that it was considered deviant behavior to demonstrate such seeming innocuous behavior as asking questions or shifting one's seat anywhere except neatly forward. One friend recounted how he was accused of talking too much or labeled a trouble maker when asking questions in class. Further, he shared how, to fit in, he tried his best to keep quiet believing that was the only way to achieve high grades in citizenship (viewed mostly as conduct that was accommodating and polite). Little did he realize this was by design; there was never an intention for him to rise to the professional or elite class where analysis, entrepreneurialism, problem finding and solving were nurtured and valued.

Hidden curriculum differs depending on social class

It is worth noting that the themes and goals of the hidden curriculum for the *middle and elite classes* are different than those for *the working and lower class*. Getting the "right" answer takes on more importance than the "right" behavior for middle class students. Middle class curriculum, with its hidden features, is one step ahead of those for the working and lower class because these students are being prepared to function on a higher social level. These more highly-regarded middle-class students are learning what's needed to direct them to white-collar jobs—management and departmental supervision roles. In school, they are expected to respond to such classroom queries as: What is the meaning of the statements made by an author? What are the steps to solving a problem? Who did what, when and why? What are other options? These students are required to exercise some level of choice—to make decisions in pursuit of discovering the right answer.

A third type of school also reflects the reality of the hidden curriculum, though based on expectations for students being tracked towards becoming affluent professionals. These students hail from upper middle class, professional families. The major theme for this group is independent creativity. Those in this echelon are expected to express, create and apply new ideas. Evaluation of students is based less on standardized test scores and grades and more on project design and development. According to Anyon, the focus for these learners is creating unique products (as expressions of their individual creativity) as an outcome of their learning and work. Clearly this is a vastly divergent goal than for students from working class families, who are only expected to use their mental muscle to find the predetermined, right answers.

Even Space Usage Matters for Hidden Curriculum Objectives

It should be noted that school space utilization, another aspect of the hidden curriculum, begins to look quite different in the affluent professional schools and more so with the fourth type, the executive elite-directed curriculum. Unlike the lower, working and middle-class schools where the teacher's desk is centered in front of the classroom with students working quietly at their individual seats neatly arranged in rows, the rising professional students work together throughout the space, either sitting or standing. The room is arranged to be more student-centered rather than teacher-centered and controlled. This spatial arrangement gives students a sense of greater control over their learning, fostering an attitude that they are ultimately responsible for what they do or do not learn.

With the fourth type of school (for executive elite students) and its hidden curriculum, the space is open, and students have free movement throughout that space. There's far less structure for the future executive elites. There are no bells to demarcate time.

So, the fourth and final type of school identified by Anyon related to "hidden curriculum" was designated as the executive elite. Most of the fathers of the children were top level executives for large corporations. There are very few if any minority children in these schools, whose families had high six-figure incomes or above. These families represent the 1% of the population that controls 20% of America's wealth. The focus for these students' education is on developing their analytical capacity.

The executive elite students are expected to systematically reason through a problem, discerning which elements are involved in the presenting problem (divergent thinking). They're then prompted

Who Dropped the Ball on our Kids? Sondai K. Lester

and required to fit those elements together in a way that offers the best solution among a range of possibilities for addressing the problem (convergent thinking). Building the capacity to critique, then form and ask good questions is embedded in the pedagogy. Disagreement with others including the teacher is accepted and expected. Asking challenging questions, in this context (unlike for lower and working class), was not only acceptable, but expected as a hallmark of intellectualism. All lessons for this group, regardless of the academic subject, centered on real life issues.

Students in this group, described by Anyon, had greater autonomy; they could come to school early to begin research, finish assignments or just read for pleasure. Examples of this type of high school, engineered to create the next generation of executive elites include such institutions as Phillip Exeter in New Hampshire, Andover in Massachusetts, St. Albans in Washington DC, and The Masters School in New York. Again, hidden in the curriculum for the executive elite school is developing the skills and aptitudes to secure a position of power and control within American society.

The essence of the intentionally delineated goals of the hidden curriculum are explicated by Anyon in this way:

> *"The analysis of differences in school work, school organization, and pedagogy in the contrasting social class context suggests that the hidden curriculum is tacit preparation for relating to the process of*

production in a specific way. Differing curricular, pedagogical and pupil evaluation practices emphasize different cognitive and behavioral skills in each educational setting. This develops in children certain potential and particular relationships to capital, authority, and the process of work based on their class position.[20]" P. 11

To summarize, the chart that follows is a snapshot of the distinctions among the four expressions of the hidden curriculum. Keep in mind, if you're a part of the Black group, the only likely way to rise above the lowest expectations is primarily through the will of parents—those parents who have not been totally victimized by their own experience, those who haven't accepted the "normalcy" of low academic achievement and status.

Hidden Curriculum's Four Expressions

Economic status	Societal expectation	Behavior expectations	Learning themes
Lower class	Laborer	Obedience, following directions	Right behavior and answer
Middle class	Managerial	Discovery	Some choice; options to find "right answer"
Upper middle class	Affluent, professional	Create, express, apply new ideas	Project design, product development
Executive elite	Positions of power and control	Analysis, reasoning, divergent and convergent thinking	Thinking "outside the box"

[20] Ibid. Anyon, J.

Who Dropped the Ball on our Kids? Sondai K. Lester

Who then should be surprised by the fact that most Black students and families occupy the bottom social and economic stations in America? What the generally low socioeconomic status reflects is that the schools, in concert with other American institutions, have been successful. The destiny of Blacks and other lower-class minority groups is both consciously and unconsciously controlled, determined, and limited by both the covert imperatives of the societally-defined social class and the racially denigrating themes embedded within the curriculum.

Make no mistake, even with the "hidden curriculum" and its social control function, how lower-class whites were to be controlled was vastly different than for Blacks. The intent was to ensure not only that class distinctions remained intact, but the racial superiority of whites (regardless of economic status) over Blacks would go undisturbed. It's no wonder the poorest, least educated white has a deep disdain for Blacks who may be at the same economic and social status as they are; they still believe deeply that they are better off by virtue of their whiteness.

Race, Class and Education

"The most potent weapon in the hands of the oppressor is the mind of the oppressed." Steve Biko

The public-school system plays a lead role in the maintenance and reproduction of the centuries-old socio-economic structure. The system brings with it all the inequities and injustices rationalized based on race, class, and ethnicity. It cannot be understated: *The school prepares students to accept and fit into the place and role in society that has been prescribed for them.* Those places and roles preserve the power relationships and system of control already in place. Speaking to the primary function of schools, Giroux and Penna state that,

> *"Instead of preparing students to enter the society with skills that will allow them to reflect critically upon and intervene in the world in order to change it, schools act as conservative forces which for the most part socialize students to conform to the status quo."*[21]

Most educational researchers who explore the conserving and reproducing function of schools have not factored in the hidden curriculum's declaration and reinforcement of white supremacy.

---

[21] Giroux, Henry and Penna, Anthony. Social education in the classroom: The dynamics of the hidden curriculum. *Theory and Research in Social Education*, V11:1, Spring 1979, P. 27

Who Dropped the Ball on our Kids? Sondai K. Lester

They've not considered the false notion that being white makes one innately intellectually superior. What was once an overt societal declaration of white intellectual superiority, and by extension cultural and moral superiority, is now tacitly incorporated within the public education curriculum. Apple[22] provides an example of how contextualizing historical events reflects this racist idea:

> "Education is deeply implicated in the politics of culture. The curriculum is never simply a neutral assemblage of knowledge, somehow appearing in the texts and classrooms of a nation. It is always part of a selective tradition, someone's selection, some group's vision of legitimate knowledge....Think of social studies texts that continue to speak of 'the Dark Ages' rather than the historically more accurate and less racist phrase 'the age of African and Asian ascendancy' or books that treat Rosa Parks as merely a naïve African-American woman who was simply too tired to go to the back of the bus, rather than discussing her training in organized civil disobedience at the Highlander Folk School."

Further Loewen[23] says it this way and within the context of the academic achievement gap between whites and minority students:

---

[22] Apple, Michael. The politics of official knowledge: Does a national curriculum make sense? *Teachers College Record* 95:2, 1993. P. 222.

[23] Loewen, James W. (1995). *Lies My Teacher Told Me: Everything Your American History Textbook Got Wrong,* New Press, NY, P. 295

Who Dropped the Ball on our Kids? Sondai K. Lester

"...the gap is largest in social studies. That is because the way American history is taught particularly alienates students of color and children from impoverished families. Feel-good history for affluent white males inevitably amounts to feel-bad history for everyone else."

This declaration of white superiority and supremacy is a pathology, a disease that is unconsciously contracted through the process of being schooled. It infects the minds, expectations and subsequently the behaviors of both Blacks and whites.

"Feel-good history for affluent white males inevitably amounts to feel-bad history for everyone else." - Loewen

While some deny it, all human interaction in this country is defined and driven by the declaration of white supremacy and Black inferiority. This devastating false assertion serves as an underpinning for school curricula. So pervasive is the conditioning of the covert (hidden) curriculum, in tandem with the reinforcing symbols and messages from the larger society, that it has become an unconscious motivator of individual behavior and cross-racial encounters. Leonard Pitts, <u>Miami Herald</u> columnist, citing the influence of education, wrote about such an encounter in an October 4, 2014 article titled, *You Almost Feel Sorry for Sean Groubert*. Groubert, a white South Carolina state trooper was fired from his job and charged with assault and battery for shooting an unarmed Black male over a seat belt violation. The dashcam video clearly shows Groubert had no apparent reason to pull his gun much less shoot the Black victim. The video shows the Black victim crying out "Why did you shoot me?" Groubert's friends were adamant in their declaration that he is not a racist. Columnist Pitts agrees that he probably is not a racist in the narrow sense in which we have come to understand racism. It seems Pitts concurs that the "hidden curriculum" to which both whites and Blacks are inculcated, grounds his understanding of the actions of the trooper. Pitts speaks of Groubert and the incident this way:

> [Groubert is] *"a citizen of a country where fear of black men is downright viral. That doesn't mean Groubert burns crosses on weekends.* **It means he's gone through school,** *watched television, seen a movie, used a computer, read a newspaper, or magazine. It means he's alive and aware in a nation where one is taught from birth that thug equals black, suspect equals black, danger equals black. It's the water we drink and the air we breathe."*

Schools, as alluded to by Pitts, like the rest of the American system, are conserving institutions with a primary function of perpetuating social systems and norms by preparing students to accept predefined positions along racial and class lines. That being true, is the low academic outcomes for a large percentage of Black students a sign of school failure or an indicator that schools have succeeded in producing the outcomes expected and defined for Black students?

Legal question of educating Blacks: To exclude or include?

The history of U.S. schooling for Black people begins with the pre-Civil War laws, particularly in the South, that strictly forbade formal education of enslaved Blacks. South Carolina, in 1740, was the first of the southern states to forbid educating enslaved Blacks. It is worth noting that the United States is believed to be the only country involved in the brutal African slave trade to disallow

---

The United States is believed to be the only European country involved in the African slave trade to *disallow* educating enslaved Blacks.

---

educating enslaved Blacks. The rationale for keeping subjugated Blacks ignorant and uneducated was that such an exclusion meant decreasing exposure to information that could incite rebellion.

Plantation owners and officials overseeing the slave-based economy espoused on one hand that Blacks were incapable of being educated, yet on the other warned that education would be a threat to white control. Carter G. Woodson, looking at the idea of educating Blacks during the chattel slave period wrote:

Who Dropped the Ball on our Kids? Sondai K. Lester

"Most southern white people reached the conclusion that it was impossible to cultivate the minds of Negroes without arousing overmuch self-assertion."[24]

So, the absence of education for Blacks was determined early on to be a means to thwart any potential to reject the system of white power and supremacy.

As Black people were slowly brought into the educational process after the early 1860s Civil War and Emancipation Proclamation, it became important to design an educational experience that was equally effective at maintaining an accepted legitimacy of white supremacy. The effort to build an educational structure for Black people formally began at the 1890 Lake Mohonk Conference in New York with the theme "The Negro Question." The year prior, this same conference had focused on ways to address Native American education. During the opening address, former President Rutherford B. Hayes, the leading influence for dismantling Reconstruction (and its reforms which had given Blacks a bit more opportunity than during legalized slavery), laid out the issue in this way:

"A century or two ago the ancestors of the great majority of the present [Negro] population of the United States were African barbarians and pagans of the lowest type. They had no skill in any

---

[24] Woodson, Carter G. (1919). *The Education of the Negro Prior to 1861*

kind of labor, nor industrious habits, and knew nothing of any printed or written language. This heathen people, brought from the Dark Continent, after several generations in bondage, followed by a few years of freedom, have all of them learned to understand and speak the English language. All of them have been taught the first, the essential lesson in civilization: They can all earn their own living by their own labor.[25]

The challenge before the conference, as outlined by Hayes, was to develop a structure and processes to enable Blacks through education to attain, in his rhetoric, the "full stature of American

> **Education for Blacks in 1890 was to be a distinctly different educational process than the one for whites.**

manhood." For Blacks, this full stature according to the conference attendees meant "teaching morality and the dignity of labor." This was to be a distinctly different educational process than the one for whites. The 1890 Conference subsequently developed four pillars that were to form the framework for designing an educational process for recently-freed Blacks. The aims were stated in this way:

1. The accomplishing of the primary education of the Negro by the states, and the further development of the means

---

[25] Shujaa, Mwalimu J., editor, (1994). *Too Much School, Too Little Education: A Paradox of Black Life in White Societies*, pg. 47

and methods to this end, until all Negroes are critically trained in primary schools,

2. The largely increased support of schools, aided by private benevolence, which shall supply teachers and preachers for the Negro race,

3. The grounding of most of these teachers and preachers in common English studies and in the English Bible, with the further opportunity for any of them to carry on their studies as far as they may desire, and

4. The great extension of industrial education for both men and women.[26]

What should be clear about the four conclusions drawn at the Conference is the expressed intention and need for whites to control the educational process for Black people. This control was solidified by providing funding, emphasizing religious study, and shaping the curriculum content. The goal was to create a segregated educational system that would teach Black people in such a way that they would acquiesce to working in the menial roles assigned to them by whites, further ensuring an acceptance of Black second-class, inferior status.

This development of a Black school system (generally segregated) was essential to the emerging industrial society's need for workers trained for the new economy's jobs. This was in sharp contrast

---

[26] Barrow, I.G., Editor (1969), *Mohonk Conference on the Negro Question*, p. 109

Who Dropped the Ball on our Kids? Sondai K. Lester

with the earlier thought that keeping Black people completely uneducated and illiterate was necessary to prevent any inclination to rebel on slave plantations.

Though clothed in pronouncements and language alluding to some higher moral good, educating Blacks ("The Negro Question") at this minimal level was an economic strategy as the country shifted from primarily an agricultural to an industrial economy near the close of the 19th Century. It also was a means

---

Educating Blacks (the late 19th century "Negro Question") at a minimal level was an economic strategy as the country shifted from an agricultural to an industrial economy, and a means to keep Blacks segregated in their social place.

---

to keep Blacks segregated and in their social place—both below and separate from whites.

The networked institutional system of racism was at work. So, while "The Negro Question" was being answered through the design of separate schooling and curriculum, during this same period, the Plessy vs. Ferguson Supreme Court case was upheld. This 1896 ruling made legal "separate but equal" and the maintenance of Jim Crow laws, continuing and deepening a generally racist environment. The case stemmed from Blacks seeking to access train seats adjacent to whites. It was part of the effort by whites to create a new societal structure that maintained white supremacy, in response to the changing dynamics between Blacks and whites post-slavery and post-Reconstruction. Plessy vs. Ferguson further legitimized the separate school systems that had already begun being established. With Blacks having unrestricted movement after the legal end of plantation containment during chattel slavery, the case was another response to: How do whites keep their dominance while keeping Blacks "in their place" without the restricted mobility ensured by their prior physical and legal enslavement?

Blacks rebel despite educational conditioning

Two decades after the Mohonk Conference, the Chicago race riot (part of the Red Summer of 1919) occurred, raising some questions about the effectiveness of the Conference attendees' aim of achieving submission through education. Here you had Black soldiers returning from World War I where they gallantly fought against fascism only to return to vigorously fight whites for Black equality in America. The Red Summer, so named because of the flow of blood from race riots in more than 30 U.S. cities, struck an irresistible chord particularly because whites were also killed and injured. This brazen resistance by Blacks raised such quandaries among whites as: Why did the educational system fail to fulfill its role of training compliance and submission into Blacks and act as a means of social control? How did Blacks schooled in

Who Dropped the Ball on our Kids? Sondai K. Lester

a white-controlled segregated public educational system develop these rebellious tendencies?

> *"What made the 1919 Chicago riot particularly interesting to whites was the fact that it was not a one-way affair in which angry white mobs killed blacks and burned down the black community. This was a confrontation in which some of the blacks fought back, and though some were killed, the fact that some white people were also killed made it imperative that some determinations be made about what was happening in the African-American community."* Shujaa, P. 51

The Chicago Commission on Race Relations subsequently commissioned a study to uncover the nature of the issues that led to the rebellions of 1919. This and other studies, were in effect, if not formally stated, efforts to understand the underlying impetus and motivators for Blacks to do the unthinkable—commit acts of violence against white authority.[27] Dr. Charles S. Johnson, a Black academic and former president of Fisk University, was commissioned by whites to lead the study. Dr. Johnson's role as a researcher (trained at the University of Chicago) was (perhaps unintentionally) to help whites probe the factors that needed to be addressed to reestablish control over the minds and actions of Black people.

---

[27] Stanfield, J. H., The ethnocentric basis of social science knowledge production, *Review of Research in Education*, 1985, 406

This rebelliousness of young Blacks was perceived as antithetical to the goals of education espoused at Mohonk and the

---

Researchers predicted a full-scale Black rebellion would occur if the segregated school system was maintained; beginning in the 1930s, the idea of desegregating the schools became a prominent theme.

---

maintenance of unquestioned white control over Blacks. The leading white intellectuals funded another study in the 1930s, under the auspices of the American Youth Commission. Its purpose was to determine the source of this rebellious behavior evidenced during the Red Summer, including the Chicago and Tulsa rebellions of 1919 and 1921 respectively. Leading Black researchers were hired, including E. Franklin Frazier, to undertake the study. The reports published by these researchers led the white elite to conclude that the segregated school system was not working in the way it was intended. They then predicted a full-scale Black rebellion would occur if the segregated school system was maintained. At the highest levels of the white establishment, beginning in the 1930s, the idea of desegregating the schools became a prominent theme.

The 1954 Brown vs. Board of Education of Topeka Supreme Court decision to mandate the desegregation of schools was a

Who Dropped the Ball on our Kids? Sondai K. Lester

direct outgrowth of the discussions begun 20 years prior (Shujaa). This was a move away from the Plessy vs. Ferguson 1896 decision as it relates to public education.

That 1954 judicial school desegregation decision was a key driver for the civil unrest and activism of Black youth. They vigorously challenged the legitimacy of the segregated system of schooling and public accommodations. While many Black activists believed America incapable of delivering education that was "separate *and* equal", many of the whites who supported integration did so because they believed separate education might incite rebellion.

Whites split over merits of school desegregation

What must be kept in mind is that the burden of desegregation (hastened by the 1954 Brown vs. Board of Education case) would be borne by poor and working-class whites who most often lived and interacted with Blacks in public spaces in low-income areas. So, the seeming split among whites regarding support of the legislation was based on economic class. The world of the white elite, who were more supportive of desegregation, was a wholly different world. Their lives were lived for the most part separate from both Blacks and whites from lower economic levels. The tension, conflict, and physical suffering that would take place was mostly between the lower echelon whites and Blacks (both groups that labored in service to the economic interests and power of the white elite). These lower level whites, largely resistant to desegregation, were fully bought in to the belief in the myth of white superiority and Black inferiority. They were blinded to the fact that they too were pawns in the system that gave the bulk of the advantages to the white elite.

The *overt* racism in America was directly expressed through the visceral often hostile interactions between lower and working-class whites and Blacks. This overt racism was a consequence of the indirectly expressed, *covert* racism of the white power elite. The elite group's power and wealth resulted from the societal systems they put in place to perpetuate white supremacy. They knew desegregating the schools would have little social effect on their exclusive lifestyles; yet the elite group depended on the working-class whites' support of white supremacy to reinforce and maintain their power over the economy.

There's a tendency to forget there's always a bigger agenda when whites offer significant support to efforts to advance the quality of life among Black people. This time, the white elite found it strategically advantageous to both support and even finance the desegregation agenda of Black activists. The "dream of integration" articulated by Dr. Martin Luther King was a concept the white elite could align with, believing it offered an avenue for Black people to be more acceptable to whites. This acceptance, they hoped, would make Blacks less of a threat to the power interests of the white elite, while the nature and power of this acceptance into America's system would continue to be defined by these elites. The desegregated school would be a symbol of this white acceptance and a source of hope for a better Black future.

The interplay of race, class and education cannot be denied when one examines the Black educational process in America. Following the chronology of educational policy over the last few centuries bears out that the belief in white supremacy and Black inferiority was and is foundational. These overarching ideas shape policy and are woven throughout all educational system change. These deeply engrained ideas will not be undone easily.

Impact of Society and Family Culture on Schooling

Culture is a powerful force for shaping behavior and expectations. Each school, home, and church along with other institutions expresses specific cultural norms and expectations. Who an individual comes to believe he or she is and what they are capable of achieving is largely culturally-determined. America's cultural norms generally adversely impact the identity of those in the oppressed group.

Families have a culture, whether or not they are consciously aware of it. Part of that culture is expressed in the nature of the relationship between the child and its parents. This relationship is the most crucial one for a developing child. The family matters because its culture can either be affirming and positively developmental or it can have devastating effect on the child's attitudes and outcomes related to education.

Culture Matters to Academic Achievement

As examined earlier, schools **conserve** and **perpetuate** the prevailing, accepted social order. How does this conserving happen? What processes are applied to induce Black students to adapt to a system that oppresses and exploits them? Why have Black educators been unable to establish schools with educational experiences that empower Black students to break free from second-class thinking and

> **Culture is a powerful force for shaping behavior and expectations.**

status? The reasons are, in part, related to Black educators' failure to analyze schooling in terms of the culture it propagates and its effect on human expectations and outcomes.

Culture is a powerful force for shaping behavior and expectations. It has been described in countless ways. Crucial to understanding its powerful imprint on education, the following two definitions are provided:

> *"Culture is the medium of personality."* –P. Bohannon, *Social Anthropology*

> *"Culture is the vast structure of behaviors, ideas, attitudes, values, habits, beliefs, customs, language, rituals, ceremonies and practices*

Who Dropped the Ball on our Kids? Sondai K. Lester

peculiar to a particular group of people which provides them with a general design for living and patterns for interpreting reality. Culture gives meaning to reality and as such has the power to compel behavior and the capacity to reinforce beliefs about self and others."[28]—*Wade Nobles*

According to Nobles, culture is *the stuff* in which human development occurs. Culture comprises the total environment. Extending the thought further, education as well as curriculum development, are cultural phenomena. Culture is an invisible, yet critical dimension of all curricula.

Most sociologists agree that the general level of expectation and performance of those within a group is culturally determined. The fundamental questions that undergird human existence and ideology formation, such as *who am I?* and more importantly, *who are we?* are answered based on the culture that defines the framework of one's life. Who an individual comes to believe he or she is and, because of that identity assessment, what they believe they are capable of achieving is culturally-determined.

---

[28] Nobles, Wade. The infusion of African and African-American content: A question of content and intent. In A. G. Hilliard, L. Payton-Stewart, and L. O. Williams (eds.), *Infusion of African and African American Content in the School Curriculum: Proceedings of the First National Conference, October 1989* (pp. 4–26).

Who Dropped the Ball on our Kids? Sondai K. Lester

When the curricular content is viewed separate from the cultural context within which the content is derived, educators and parents alike are stymied in their ability to positively impact outcomes for Black children. As an example, to this day I have a vivid, disturbing mental image of my elementary school's talent show. The song "Me and My Shadow" was enacted, with one of my Black classmates trailing behind the white lead singer as his shadow. It was a pitiful, yet remarkably powerful sight. It seemed not a parent, not even mine, was struck by this identity shaping and reinforcing imagery—a white child singing and walking along as the Black shadow mimicked his every move. Everyone took for granted that this was how it was supposed to be—isn't a shadow dark? Yet the perpetuation of Black as *less than* was there in that classroom culture as the parents—Black and white—smiled with pride and agreement. In the same vein, why did my parents find it unremarkable that I went from kindergarten through high school without ever having a single teacher who looked like me? This reinforced that those leading us are white and those likely to be not much more than shadows in our community, look like me. It

> **Who an individual comes to believe he or she is and what they believe they are capable of achieving is largely culturally-determined.**

must not be forgotten that, as Dr Dubois memorably stated, "education is always and everywhere political."

Mw. J. Shujaa further illuminates the power of school culture:

> *"Schooling exerts an influence on individual achievement expectations through its policies, e.g., tracking, culturally biased standardized tests, grade-based reward system and awarding of credentials that lead to inclusion of some as successful and exclusion of most others. These policies are affirmed and reinforced by the larger social structure." p. 17*

School policies are important expressions and validation of the culture the school promotes, and they reflect the underlying assumptions built into the curriculum that informs what students learn. How do school curriculum leaders glaringly omit the centuries of the brutal transatlantic slave trade—a Black holocaust—from the certified text books, when addressing how America was built? It's a conscious choice.

What is imperative for educators' consideration, when dealing with the issue of building an effective educational experience for Black students, is that **culture is a vehicle through which the oppressor controls the minds and behaviors of the oppressed**. The school is an essential element in the societal infrastructure through which cultural norms and standards are transmitted. In a discriminatory society based on the oppression of one group by another, culture is the means through which that power discrepancy is sustained. We should not be stunned that African Centered Education (which was mandated for the Detroit Public School system in 1994) was disparaged after a time. Its ideology ran counter to the larger and dominant culture's norms. American schools, by their very nature, are expected to reinforce the status quo. Why hasn't Black history and cultural study maintained a place in the education of new generations (post 1970s and 1980s) of Black students? Why is Maulana Karenga's Kwanzaa model for African-American community-building only marginally acknowledged or seen as a fad? Infusion of these ideas is off-script as they relate to America's intent to educate Blacks in a way that ensures we maintain our lower-class places in society.

The goal of the powerful economic elites is to assimilate the oppressed into the status quo by "educating" them to identify with the culture of their oppressor, thereby gaining their unconscious cooperation in the maintenance of the oppressive system. The generally low academic performance by most Black and other youth of color can be directly linked to the quality of identity formation promoted by the schools. It is well-known that self-concept and self-esteem are social constructions that the school has a critical role in shaping. The public schools, as an extension of white western culture, sanctions a curriculum that has both explicitly and implicitly reinforced the concept of white supremacy and Black inferiority. The Eurocentric perspective (an

Who Dropped the Ball on our Kids? Sondai K. Lester

interpretation of history and culture slanted towards European values and experiences), at the core of the curriculum, justifies the power discrepancy between races and is skillfully threaded throughout the schools' coursework. The Eurocentric-based mandated school courses have worked in concert with other social institutions (religious, political, judicial, etc.) to instill an abnormal Black pathological personality. This systems approach ensures the maintenance of a Black condition of second-class citizenship.

> **The Eurocentric view of history and culture (slanted towards European values and experiences) is at the core of the curriculum. It justifies the power differential between races and is skillfully threaded throughout the schools' coursework.**

Contrast the opposing psychological effects of Black students embracing an Afrocentric viewpoint over 12 to 16 years of schooling. Matriculating through a curriculum undergirded by a philosophy of collectivism and racial self-pride would have a different effect. Grounded in the triumphs and trials of one's own ancient and recent ancestral experience, this educational foundation would likely lead to a heightened, positive view of the Black group and community consciousness. The table that follows shows the contrasting views of history and their effects on identity formation. Sadly, the Afrocentric view is largely nonexistent in K-

12 public schools and universities. The western worldview is not only embraced by Blacks in America but also those on the African continent and in the Caribbean islands. Case in point: A recent visit to West Africa's Ghana, popularly called the gateway to the African Motherland, highlighted the white-washing of Black African culture. Nearly every block in the major cities were strewn with images of a white Jesus, advertisements for bleaching creams, waist thinners and weaves, and a good number of streets were named after famous white Americans. Without question, large populations in these African diaspora regions have also faced relentless psychic assault and indoctrination through western education because these regions are also outposts for white control of wealth.

Dimensions of history[29]	Eurocentric view	Afro-centric view
Time dimension	Recent	Ancient
Location of origin	Western world	Eastern world
General ethos	I-centered	We-centered
Behavioral norms	Competition, self-interest, individualism	Cooperation, group interest, communalism
Typical social effects	Alienation, distrust, loneliness	Belonging, interdependence
Religion	Ideas/strict dogma	Experiential/spiritualism

[29] Lester, Sondai and Lindiwe (1998), *Connections Remembered*, Vol. 1, p. 16

Who Dropped the Ball on our Kids? Sondai K. Lester

Blacks "brain damaged" by American schooling

The late Amos Wilson, former professor of psychology at Morehouse College, pointed out that being programmed (through a racially-deflating external environment) to believe in the idea of white supremacy and Black inferiority has led to a form of *brain damage* among Black people. Wilson[30] builds on Ashley Montagu's concept of sociogenic brain damage, which occurs due to deprivation of the social stimulation needed for the brain to function optimally. This is not much different from the idea that deprivation of proper dietary nutrients leads to a breakdown in physical development.

Montagu's research on brain development points out the critical effect of external influences on the brain's functioning during the first three years of life. Unlike most species, humans are born before the brain has completed its development. Once born, a child's essential neural connections begin to take shape. The brain undergoes a dramatic increase in size during these first few years of life, greatly affected by the complexity and density of the neural connections it is making. These connections are made in response to the type of stimulation the child receives from the external environment. The richer the environmental stimuli, the denser

---

[30] Wilson, Amos. (1978). *The Developmental Psychology of the Black Child*

Who Dropped the Ball on our Kids? Sondai K. Lester

and more complex the neural connections, and as such the greater the child's cognitive capacity.

Social-cultural deficiencies then can have an adverse effect on the brain. Montagu believes these environmental insufficiencies can lead to what he terms **social deprivation syndrome**.[31] Two of the syndrome's hallmarks are **shortened attention span and difficulty learning**. These connect directly to low test scores and generally low school performance. The implications are staggering for Black children. Socially-deprived infants and preschoolers (up to age 3) will very likely have brain wiring that translates into negative or less than optimal identity formation.

Imagine the Black infant born into a household which has faced generational poverty and other strifes. Despite the parents' best efforts to break that cycle, there is little chance of having the time or mental space to expose the child to a range of books, consistent positive feedback, and messages of hope about the world's promises for him or her. The child is not likely to be privy to, without tremendous effort, positive, redeeming Black images either through media or by peering out the window into his or her physical surroundings. Where does a struggling Black parent—trying to make ends meet, a victim of discriminatory, low quality housing, with a low-paying job—find the time, the will and

---

[31] Montagu, Ashley, (1974) *Culture and Human Development: Insight into Growing Human.* Prentice Hall.

Who Dropped the Ball on our Kids? Sondai K. Lester

mindset to say: "I've got to be sure my child has ample engagement and experiences with a positive environment—one vibrant with color, options, books, games, smiles, supportive adults, etc."? Well, God bless those who do. Because it takes all the strength a Black parent can muster to create a path for their child in the face of the low expectations already set for the child by the culture of oppression, embodied in the economic system and the schools. It's no simple accomplishment for parents in a socially deprived environment to raise children who break through these visible and invisible barriers erected on every side!

Amos Wilson coined his own phrase similar to Montagu's— **psychogenic brain damage**. He posits that a human brain existing within an impoverished environment is adversely affected. By being constantly exposed to hostile or self-negating environmental stimuli, neural connections are built that not only have a detrimental impact on the brain's ability to function but also on one's mindset, one's consciousness. Such an environment will actually deepen and reinforce a self-negating identity. The damaged brain that results from the socially-deprived setting will make it difficult for the individual to engage in behavior opposed to that socially conditioned identity. The Black child's brain stricken with psychogenic damage cannot process or conform to ideas that run counter to the dominant culture's negative view on Black people's human worth and value.

Again, imagine the same infant from the deprived physical environment at age five. Visualize her opening Christmas presents with two dolls among them, one white and one Black. Imagine her frowning at the Black toy, then immediately showing delight when opening the gift with the white one inside (a common occurrence). How do you explain that so early in life? How is it that when the doll looks like an image of the child, she wants no part of it? This discouraging and revelatory phenomenon, uncovered by Drs. Kenneth and Mamie Clark in their 1939 doll study, was re-confirmed when the study was repeated in 2005. Harlem high school student Kiri Davis conducted her study to find the same exact outcomes. Then, Professor Margaret Beale Spencer in 2010 validated the same preferences for a CNN report. The latter two studies re-established the devastating durability of this self-negating brain damage. The continuing bias towards whiteness on the part of both white and Black children indicates, says Professor Spencer, *"We are still living in a society where dark things are devalued, and white things are valued."*[32]

> **How is it that when the doll looks like an image of the Black child, she wants no part of it? "We are still living in a society where dark things are devalued, and white things are valued."**

---

[32] Study: White and black children biased toward lighter skin, CNN, May 14, 2010, accessed at cnn.com. Contributors: Jill Billante and Chuck Hadad

Who Dropped the Ball on our Kids? Sondai K. Lester

Unfortunately, most Black people live in physical and economic conditions that deny them (whether deliberate or due to benign neglect) experiences that affirm their innate racial human equality. Demographers consistently show Black people near or at the bottom of the statistical strata related to housing, education, health, well-being, incarceration rates, etc. Consequently, most of our people suffer from social deprivation syndrome and thus, are likely to develop an identity that reinforces second-class status.

Montagu's notion of social deprivation syndrome and Wilson's closely-related psychogenic brain damage theory are reminders of Dr. Carter G. Woodson's view on the negative identity issues related to public education. He articulated it nearly 100 years ago in The Mis-education of the Negro (1933) in this way:

> "No systematic effort toward change has been possible, for taught the same economics, history, philosophy, literature, and religion which have established the present code of morals, the Negro's mind has been brought under the control of his oppressor. The problem of

When you control a man's thinking you do not have worry about his actions.

> holding the Negro down, therefore, is easily solved. When you control a man's thinking you do not have to worry about his actions. You do not have to tell him not to stand here and go yonder. He will find

Who Dropped the Ball on our Kids? Sondai K. Lester

*his proper place and will stay in it. You do not need to send him to the back door. He will go without being told. In fact, **if there is no back door, he will cut one for his special benefit. His education makes it necessary.**"* P. xiii

The public schools are an extension of white western culture and a major instrument of socialization. The schools have a deeply infused Euro-centric curriculum which has both explicitly and implicitly ingeniously threaded a theme of Black inferiority throughout that curriculum. The white-washed literature and social science content areas, both crucial to identity formation, lead the Black child inevitably to arrive at **several self-negating conclusions, including**:

✓ **Black people are intellectually less capable than whites** (given the paucity if not complete absence of Black voices contributing to these content areas)

✓ **There is little value in learning about the Black historical experience** because the only credible world view is Euro-centric (validated by "learned" white scholars who tell the human story—both historical and contemporary— through the white western perspective).

✓ **The normal psychology for a Black child is one of mental submission** to the idea that their second-class status is natural, right, historical and irrevocable. (This happens as an outcome of being bombarded and assaulted—from as early as pre-school in and outside of the classroom—with ideas and images of diminished worth and value of Black people).

✓ **Low academic outcomes for Black students are expected and accepted.** (Test scores, high school and college completion rates far below national norms are signs of the school's success not failure, in that they confirm what the white world declared—Blacks are inferior in every way.)

Quick trip from feeling equal to "less than"

"Like flowers planted in the sun, we too can give forth blossoms, shared by everyone." —Langston Hughes, from the poem Some Day

A Black child is born into the world with the innate capacity to perform at equally high levels as that of a child from any other racial or ethnic group. We see examples of Hughes' beautiful, bounteous blossoms in the amazing accomplishments of Black individuals who have been exposed to supportive, challenging environments. These have broken through the onslaught of "you can't" images, proclamations, laws and institutional systems. From school leaders to scientists to athletes to artists; from corporate leaders, school academies with 100% of the students college-ready and college bound, entertainers to president, we have exemplars in every field demonstrating our capacity to fully bloom.

These accomplished, barrier-busting individuals certainly are positive models, yet they remain anomalies because the basic notion that Black people are equal and have the potential for excellence conflicts with the cultural premise of Black racial inferiority declared by the dominant American culture. Schools are co-conspirators in this diminishing of the Black child because it takes on the role of socializing and rewiring the "blossom potential" into a weed with an identity that is aligned with their lower social station. The school's mandate, in reality, is to "educate" the child to function in opposition to its innate striving for wholeness, power and human equality. Eventually it becomes too exhausting to believe he or she is "powerful beyond measure" as Nelson Mandela reminded us. **There is likely a pivotal moment of resignation**—when the child settles in and becomes someone other than who he or she really is and could become. Those who break out of this matrix, resisting this assault on self, are subject to their voices being systematically silences (including using violent means). These are our Denmark Veseys, Marcus Garveys, Angela Davis's, Patrice Lumumbas, Kathleen Cleavers, and Fred Hamptons.

As the Black child becomes aware of the intensifying conflict between society's definition of the Black self and his or her true self, this struggle becomes the source of an abnormal psychology and intense psychic pain. Dubois in his 1903 <u>The Souls of Black Folks</u> described this painful inner conflict:

> *"It is a peculiar sensation, this double consciousness, this sense of always looking at oneself through the eyes of others, of measuring one's soul by the tape of the world that looks on in amazed contempt and pity. One ever feels his twoness—an American, a Negro; two warring souls, two thoughts, two unreconciled strivings; two warring ideas in one dark body—whose dogged strength alone keeps it from being torn asunder."*

All too often, even with dogged will, exhaustion at swimming against the powerful tide sets in and with it an inability to maintain some semblance of wholeness. Many Black people become psychologically debilitated from the weight of it. This disorder finds expression in many ways including chronic depression and feelings of utter helplessness in the face of life's challenges. It also shows up through escaping into a world of fantasy and self-delusion with no connection to the real world. Others, more successful at navigating the chronic state of

Are we the only ones that require two ways of being, making peace with Dubois' notion of double-consciousness?

institutional oppression, become adept at *code-switching*, shifting language, intonation and style to be more acceptable to whites—by "being Black and speaking white" with the hope of acceptance. Are we the only ones that require two ways of being, of making peace with Dubois' notion of double-consciousness?

Once a Black child becomes psychologically overwhelmed and controlled by this inferiorized, other self, the child experiences a diminished capacity to believe he can soar academically. He avoids rigorous academic content (or is steered away from it by school counselors). Malcolm X recounts this derailing of his academic potential in his writings. He was dissuaded from studying law despite being a top student in his school. His teacher's response to his aspirations in the legal field was: "That's no realistic goal for a nigger."[33] Once our children (who've been effectively conditioned to low expectations throughout their school tenure) leave school with a diploma or as a dropout, they are found to be unprepared to function in society except at the lowest levels (for which they have been successfully prepared!). Shujaa[34] terms this generalized pattern of education that diminishes the potential of the masses of Black people "diseducation," leading to achieving at low levels, far beneath a Black child's capacity.

---

[33] Cited in Coates, Ta-Nehisi (2017). *We Were Eight Years in Power*, p. 72
[34] Shujaa, Mwalimu J., Editor, (1994). *Too Much School, Too Little Education: A Paradox of Black Life in White Societies*, p. 45

Sociologist Claude Steele has analyzed this failure to comparably achieve when looking at academic disparities between white and Black students[35]. He posits that the discrepancy exists because society generally devalues the capacity of Black young people. It grows out of the torrent of images that bombard Black children on every side. By and large, these images send the message that they have limited human worth and capacity to achieve at high levels. Steele explains that Blacks face a double devaluation related to education:

> *These images do something as well, something especially pernicious in the classroom. They set up a jeopardy of double devaluation for blacks, a jeopardy that does not apply to whites. Like anyone, blacks risk devaluation for a particular incompetence such as a failed test or flubbed pronunciation, but they further risk that such performances will confirm the broader racial inferiority they are suspected of. Thus, from the first grade through graduate school, blacks have the extra fear that in the eyes of those around them their full humanity could fall with a poor answer or a mistaken stroke of the pen. P. 73-74*

He further asserts that many Black students learn to protect themselves psychologically from this double devaluation by disidentifying with school as a source of self-esteem. This

---

[35] Steele, Claude. Race and the schooling of Black Americans. *Atlantic Monthly, April 1992.*

Who Dropped the Ball on our Kids? Sondai K. Lester

disidentification with school and "diseducation" go hand in hand, with this convergence often leading to dismal outcomes. Because they are not fully connected or have "checked out" of education as a source of affirming identity, the system largely ignores them or views them as a menace. Many high-talent Black students have been victims of this double devaluation, with the school message systems and school teachers as the arbiters. Ultimately these checked out students are not prepared to achieve in the traditional ways society defines as expressions of success.

Certainly however, there are exceptions to this low-expectations "diseducation," particularly among the Black middle class. Here we get a glimpse of the nature of "miseducation" rather than "diseducation."

"Miseducation" of the Black elite

Some children, because of certain environmental circumstances, can disconnect themselves from any personal link to the Black group. They seek high achievement while disavowing any racial affiliation. These children as adults, firmly entrenched in viewing the world through the eyes of their oppressor, tend to disown any identification with or responsibility for the plight of Black people. They are not likely to give a "leg up" to their brethren. They revel in being the "only" at their level of organizational achievement. They are indeed the "company man" or woman. They sense more commonality and association with the oppressor than the oppressed, until the white power group delivers a rude awakening. That's the moment of truth which they'd fought hard to escape—that they are in the same boat as the rest of the Black folks.

This "enlightened elite" segment of the Black population illuminates the far-reaching effects of being *miseducated*. Coming to terms with the challenge of America's Black students requires recognition that there are two levels of educational segmentation. First, there's the "diseducation" of African American students, characterized by the chronic low academic levels as measured by standardized tests, literacy scores, and graduation rates. This lack of fundamental skills and knowledge keeps this segment of the Black community trapped on the economic margins of society in low paying, dead-end jobs.

Besides "diseducation," the other level explicated by Dr. Woodson (and others) is the "miseducation" of the Black middle class. Children from these households grow up in an environment that nurtures high academic achievement. Their parents have at least graduated from high school and in most cases have had some degree of post-secondary education. They've likely attained well-paying jobs that afford the luxuries of a middle-class lifestyle. Their "miseducation" is based on the development of a psychological pathology (including disowning their historical Black culture) that leads them to identify with the oppressor's world and ideas. They seek flight from the masses and continually

Who Dropped the Ball on our Kids? Sondai K. Lester

strive for integration into the white world as a symbol of success and worth.

Dubois' concept of two warring souls within one Black body then becomes more complex and problematic. It leads to a conflict between the Black masses fighting for survival and wholeness in a racist world and the conditioned Black educated middle class's effort to deny any connection to that larger Black reality. Notes Dubois in 1939:

> *"One of the most striking evidences of the failure of higher education among Negroes is their estrangement from the masses, the very people upon whom they must eventually count on for carrying out a program of progress."* p. 52

Those in the Black middle class do not navigate the white world unscathed, even when they cling to the illusion that America is color-blind. On the one hand, the Black masses suffer a psychological and physical victimization that is culturally based. On the other, those who are part of the educated Black middle class experience a racially-based psychological victimization, which has a damaging effect on the efforts of Blacks to escape oppression. The damage also has a psychic effect on the Black intellectual. It shows itself when they must face the reality of their "sameness" in the eyes of whites. Carter G. Woodson described this conundrum facing the Black intellectual in his early 20th century writing:

"The only question which concerns us here is whether these educated persons are actually equipped to face the ordeal before them or unconsciously contribute to their own undoing by perpetuating the regime of the oppressor.[36]" Xxxi

Further, Woodson conveys this detrimental effect on the educated Black elite in his often-quoted passage:

"The same educational process which inspires and stimulates the oppressor with the thought that he is everything and has accomplished everything worthwhile, depresses and crushes at the same time the spark of genius in the Negro by making him feel that his race does not amount to much and never will measure up to the standards of other people. The Negro thus educated is a hopeless liability to his race." p. xiii

E. Franklin Frazier, Harold Cruse, Franz Fanon and Nathan Hare have all written about this intellectual crippling of the Black middle class. Much of the hope of an oppressed group is tied to the capacity and willingness of its educated, i.e., Dubois's Talented Tenth, to access, deploy and manage the strategies and processes necessary for the group to escape oppression. Unfortunately, that hope is often squashed when the educated class fails to deliver, opting instead for personal assimilation into the dominant culture.

---

[36] Woodson, Carter G. (1933). Mis-education of the Negro. Associated Publishers.

Who Dropped the Ball on our Kids? Sondai K. Lester

Frazier, in his last published essay, *The Failure of the Negro Intellectual* in 1962, describes this as a pathological drive among the Black middle class to assimilate into the white world. Assimilation, he says, refers to complete identification with the people and culture of the larger dominant community. The deeper and more complete the feeling of racial inferiority and the insecurities born of self-hatred, the stronger the drive to assimilate. In essence, it means becoming racially invisible. Says Frazier:

> *"The truth of the matter is that for most Negro intellectuals the integration of the Negro masses means the emptying of his life of meaningful content and ridding him of all Negro identification. For them, integration and eventual assimilation, means the annihilation of the Negro—physically, culturally and spiritually."* P. 7

Fundamentally, according to Frazier, the real failure of the Black intellectual is the failure to accept responsibility for providing a means for Black positive racial identity through lifting up Black history, literature, art, music and drama. If the oppressed cannot break free from an identity tied to a belief in a myth of their inferiority, they will lack the intellectual and psychological capacity to commit themselves to struggling to break free of their second-class condition. That struggle requires a perspective on their identity that contradicts that of their oppressor.

Who Dropped the Ball on our Kids? Sondai K. Lester

The Black educated elite too often act as co-conspirators with the dominant white group in preserving a system that demeans, subjugates, and exploits the masses of Black people based on skin color. They function as *gatekeepers*—deciding who among the oppressed masses are worthy of a status that allows them an illusion of acceptance into the white world. They do this because they too are psychologically imprisoned and scarred by a culture of unrelenting Black subjugation.

Reflecting back on Wade Nobles definition of culture, that says it "gives meaning to reality and as such has the power to compel behavior,"

The typical Black personality and associated behaviors are cultural creations.

the typical Black personality and associated behaviors are cultural creations. So, culture matters! In the case of education, school culture acts as a powerful instrument to shape personality and behavior. To a greater or lesser degree, all Black people think and act in ways that conform to the white declaration of Black inferiority. This is glaringly apparent, whether through expectation of a lower social place; unwavering commitment to white cultural norms, symbols and holidays; giving the benefit of the doubt to whites while offering no preferential attitudes towards one's own people; or through lack of support of quality Black businesses. The culturally-conditioned pathological Black personality causes Black parents and children to unconsciously conspire to undermine the possibility of achieving at the highest academic levels.

To ameliorate the challenges of educating Black children in American schools, which are grounded in the myth of Black inferiority, requires we consider the household and family environment along with the schools. These familial settings either provide an environment to support low expectations and "diseducation" or they can serve as countervailing forces to help recover and more fully develop the Black child's wholeness. A brief look at the Black family's role in the education of our children follows.

Family Matters in the Racial Achievement Gap

The primary challenge facing Black parents in American society is developing within their children a positive racial identity. This is particularly onerous given the onslaught of societal influences designed to undermine their healthy Black identity. Schools are not safe havens against these negative societal influences; they are part of it. Most African American parents make the faulty assumption that schools exist to make their children literate and build competencies to become successful adults. The truth is: The function of the school is to prepare students to accept their place and assigned status prescribed by the larger society. The schools reproduce the historical divisions and group positioning based on race and class.

A Black child is dependent upon her parents to establish a foundation for a healthy, affirming Black identity before entering the school. The child's home environment (culture) must be both a reflection and reinforcement of a Black self that is fully capable of achieving at the highest levels possible. The building of a positive racial self-image must be nurtured alongside the development of competencies necessary for academic success.

Yet, Black families have a long way to go to be the needed seedbed for our children's early development of positive self-identity. (The

Who Dropped the Ball on our Kids? Sondai K. Lester

parents' own experience cannot be dismissed. They have suffered decades of being diminished by the social institutions and culture of oppression from childhood up to the time they became parents. Consider again the re-administered 1939 doll study:

> *"The reassuring female voice asks the child a question—'Can you show the doll that looks bad?' The child, a pre-school aged Black girl, quickly picks up and shows the Black doll over a White one that is identical in every respect except complexion...'And why does she look bad?' 'Because she is Black', the girl answers emphatically."*[37]

High schooler Kiri Davis, in 2005, indicates these negative racial perceptions had already begun taking hold among preschoolers. Fifteen of the 21 children at the Harlem Daycare Center, where Davis conducted the study, preferred the white doll. These youngsters, between ages three and seven, had hardly been outside of their households. So, what's happening in those households for these Black children to have already taken on the self-negating attitudes of the dominant society?

Relationships in the home matter

Martin Buber, the late Jewish philosopher, declared that "in the beginning is the relationship." The most crucial relationship for a

---

[37] Edney, Hazel Trice, <u>National News</u>, New "doll test" produces ugly results. 9/14/2006.

child is the one between the child and its parents. Between birth and age five the foundations for cognition, personality and identity are laid. It is the parents who have the primary control over the environment that initially is the basis for establishing these foundations.

Black adults, based on generational conditioning to America's racist declaration of Black inferiority, have already spent their own lifetimes being conditioned to feel shame about their external "dark" appearance. They've had it hammered into their psyche that Blackness is a symbol of inadequacy. As they begin parenting, often without awareness, they are supporting messages from the larger society within their homes, imprinting a badge of racial inferiority upon their children. They set up a home environment based on the norms, values and expectations that lead the child into conformity—rather than resistance—to the status quo of second-class citizenship.

The typical Black household, especially when controlling for income (with systemic racism ensuring high percentages are trapped below the poverty line), has a structure that is designed to make it almost impossible to achieve at academic levels—comparable to that of white students attending top suburban schools. What happens in these households that is severely limiting the Black child to achieve academically? What are parents

Who Dropped the Ball on our Kids? Sondai K. Lester

doing or unconsciously not doing to foster this troubling, race-negating home culture?

President Barack Obama, speaking at the NAACP centennial celebration in 2009 said:

> *"Government programs alone won't get our children to the promised land. We need a new mindset, a new set of attitudes—because one of the most durable and destructive legacies of racial discrimination is the way we have internalized a sense of limitation—how so many in our community have come to expect so little of ourselves."*

Tom Burrell, in his book *Brainwashed*[38], which analyzes the impact of the white myth of Black inferiority on Black life, says: "We have been infected by an internalized sense of limitation." This sense

"We have been infected by an internalized sense of limitation."- Burrell

of limitation, based on our skin color, is culturally derived and perpetuated through the institutional network, including the family. This constrained sense of possibility partially accounts for the generally low expectations for Black students' educational outcomes.

---

[38] Burrell, Tom (2010). *Brainwashed: Challenging the Myth of Black Inferiority.*

How do Black parents help their children circumvent all the forces arrayed against them? Many forces are intent on them accepting the societally-constructed limitations based on their skin color. In a recent television interview with Michelle Obama and a group of Detroit area Black male college students, they expressed their frustration at the belief held by whites that they were only in college because of affirmative action; not because they had the ability to succeed. The home environment must be set up in such a way as to bolster their confidence and will to achieve to their potential despite the pressure to fail. What, then, are some elements of a home environment that affirm a positive racial identity and self-image? There are several areas a Black family must emphasize to answer these queries. These include, but are not limited to, broad areas of **identity shaping influences in the home,** such as:

1. setting up an affirming physical environment (replete with pictures, books, artifacts),
2. exposing children to cultural experiences, e.g., museums, plays, movies (focused on historic and current themes)
3. engaging in conversations about race and identity (historic foundations and contemporary themes), and
4. modeling behaviors that reflect the values of love, concern and responsibility for one another and the larger community, e.g., volunteering, community service, assisting and supporting neighbors.

Who Dropped the Ball on our Kids? Sondai K. Lester

Along with creating a home environment that can lead to a deeply rooted positive racial self-image, the parents must also assist their children in building the competencies necessary to thrive in the world by succeeding academically. This is not an undertaking that happens without forethought and conscious, ongoing effort.

The challenge for Black parents, in creating a racially wholesome place to raise children, is that parents forget that they too have been systematically contaminated by this same destructive mindset. Parents have need to remain vigilant and keep fighting their own fears, low expectations, and diminished self-esteem –all conditioned into them over their lifetimes. Without that awareness, many Black parents begin the parenting journey with an unspoken assumption that their children cannot achieve at high levels. The Black household becomes an environment that prepares children to function at lower (or, with effort, average) academic levels. Those households, despite good intention, set up a structure and relationships (a culture) that unintentionally thwart the development of the competencies needed to be successful in school. What do these kinds of home behaviors, attitudes and structures look like? Reginald Clark, over 30 years ago, in *Family Life and School Achievement*[39] helps answer that question. He says the biggest barriers to high academic achievement faced by Black families is not poverty, single-parent households or uneducated

---

[39] Clark, Reginald (1984). *Family Life and School Achievement: Why Poor Black Children Succeed or Fail.*

Who Dropped the Ball on our Kids? Sondai K. Lester

parents. The biggest factor is the culture of the home. He identified **some of the characteristics of homes that produce low-achieving students**:

- ✓ Limited parent involvement and interest in a child's home activities
- ✓ Limited parent/child activities involving literacy tasks, e.g., studying, reading, and writing; information sharing and creating
- ✓ Limited parental teaching, advising, and demonstrating concepts and ideas to children
- ✓ Inconsistent or non-existent parental guidelines and expectations for behavior in school and neighborhood settings
- ✓ Frequent criticism (deficit-based reinforcement) about a child's worth or ability

Tom Burrell, author of *Brainwashed*, further identifies factors in the interaction between parent and child that limit a Black child's likelihood for school success:

1. **Fear of failure**—Out of fear or their own personal sense of inadequacy, parents often stifle a child's desire to select challenging curriculums. This fear of failure promotes a *why even try?* attitude and often causes a parent and child to accept academic mediocrity, what Burrell refers to as *Ds will do syndrome.*

Who Dropped the Ball on our Kids? Sondai K. Lester

2. **Misguided protection**—Black parents who want their children to feel good about themselves go out of their way to protect them from failure, especially as it relates to academics. This defense mechanism prevents a child from getting involved in rigorous academic content that requires the capacity to deal with failure.

3. **Success neurosis**—Black children are often discouraged, by parents and friends, from aspiring and achieving at levels higher than "the group" so as not to be ostracized or stigmatized by other youth as *stuck up* or *acting white*.

4. They do not present to their children **counter-arguments** to the daily dosage of ideas and images that reinforce white supremacy and Black inferiority.

5. They provide their children with **objects** and images that reflect white as the standard for beauty and all that's good.

Language development gap in the home

"Did you know that the achievement gap is really a vocabulary gap that starts when kids are eighteen months old?"[40] Catherine Snow

"From the time they are born until they enter school, children need to be bathed in love and language." –Paul Lawrence[41]

---

[40]From Literacy to learning: An interview with Catherine Snow. *Harvard Education Review*, July-August 2005

[41] Cited in Bardige, Betty (2005). *At a Loss for Words: How America is Failing our children and What We Can Do About it*

The language used by the family and within the household directly affects academic outcomes. Why? Because literacy, foundational language mastery (not just the ability to read), is crucial to academic success. Betty Hart and Todd Risley from the University of Kansas undertook a study on racial literacy gaps. They published the results in *Meaningful Differences*.[42] The authors sought to more deeply grasp the reason for the persistent race and class-based achievement gap despite the countless interventions that came out of the mid-1960s War on Poverty. A group of Kansas urban community leaders worked with the university professors to examine the problem. The researchers observed the literacy experience of children, specifically spontaneous speech, from birth to five years of age based on socio-economic status as a factor contributing to the achievement disparity.

They compared the spontaneous speech (i.e., speech that happens naturally without being prompted with questions) of pre-school children in the Juniper Gardens housing development with that of the university's laboratory preschoolers (children of professors). They observed that most of the **preschoolers parented by the professors:**

1. verbalized more than twice as much,

---

[42] Hart, B. and Risley, T. (1995) *Meaningful Differences in the Everyday Life of Children.*

Who Dropped the Ball on our Kids? Sondai K. Lester

2. talked about a wider range of aspects related to what they were doing, and

3. posed more questions to figure out how and why things worked, when compared with the Juniper children.

Of even greater concern was the flatter vocabulary growth curve for the Juniper Gardens children compared to the professors' children of the same age. This growth curve widened over time, so that by the time the children entered kindergarten there was a wide gap in the vocabulary accessible to each group. By high school, the children from families in the lowest income brackets lacked the vocabulary used in the more advanced textbooks. **Vocabulary growth rates are strongly associated with rates of cognitive growth**; meaning, limited vocabulary limits learning.

The following tables illustrates the vocabulary disparity from birth to age five based on socio-economic status discovered by Hart and Risley. This sheds light on how critical what happens in the home is to preparing children to learn. What we gather from the data is that those from the lowest socio-economic rung suffer a double whammy when it comes to language and future educational success. The lower the economic status, the fewer words learned when compared to children from families higher on the economic ladder. In addition, and deeply disappointing, the words these preschoolers hear are more negative and discouraging than positive and encouraging. This reinforces the image that

Who Dropped the Ball on our Kids? Sondai K. Lester

being Black means being "less than." Study the charts carefully; they can provide hints for making positive changes in the home.

NUMBER OF WORDS LEARNED (birth to age three)

Socio-economic status	Total number of vocabulary words	Words added between critical 30th to 36th month
Professional	1200	350
Working class	700	200
On federal or state assistance	500	168

NUMBER OF WORDS HEARD BY AGE FOUR

Socio-economic status	Heard weekly through parent/child interactions	Cumulative word experience
Professional	215,000	45 million
Working class	125,000	26 million
On federal or state assistance	62,000	13 million

Tone of conversation between parents and children-TYPES OF WORDS HEARD PER HOUR

Socio-economic status	Types and tone of conversations
Professional	32 affirmatives/encouragements v. 6 prohibitions/discouragements
Working class	12 affirmatives/encouragements v. 7 prohibitions/discouragements
On federal or state assistance	5 affirmatives/encouragements v. 11 prohibitions/discouragements

Who Dropped the Ball on our Kids? Sondai K. Lester

These vocabulary and subsequent cognitive gaps cannot be rationalized based on genetic or hereditary factors. They related more to patterns transmitted across generations among families living in poverty (Hart and Risley). Or to be completely forthright

> **This self-negating cultural transmission was and is imposed and reinforced through a complex institutional network of oppression.**

as it relates to the Black experience, it can be accounted for in the **transmission of a culture of oppression across generations** since the time of chattel slavery. This adverse, self-negating cultural transmission was and is imposed and reinforced through a complex institutional network of oppression.

Within this culture, the home of most Black children lacks language richness, thus is deficient in stimulating a desire for continually learning new words necessary to comprehend and navigate the changing world. The Black child tends to be raised in a language impoverished environment characterized by "basic survival" or coping conversations with a high number of interactions fraught with anger and frustration between adults and children. These interactions, noted by Hart and Risley, were more often pointing out the child's unacceptable behaviors.

Who Dropped the Ball on our Kids? Sondai K. Lester

While the research is startling, it is at the same time instructive. It points towards at least one strategy to improve the chances for Black children from difficult socio-economic circumstances to attain higher academic performance. Changing the language exposure and patterns in the home can yield transformative results. While we have a lot to contend with as we raise our children, if families and preschool programs just emphasized Black children's language exposure and development, there would be great progress! For example, even these three simple actions on the part of parents and teachers can be differentiators:

> **Changing a child's language exposure and patterns in the home can yield transformative results.**

1. **Talk more** to your children
2. Intentionally **speak more affirmatively** around the home
3. Provide **more reading material**

These seeming small actions remind me about growing up reading comic books. My father would bring them home for me each week. I hadn't consciously thought, and maybe neither did he, that he was shaping my reading and thinking habits for a lifetime by exposing me to vocabulary and human experience stories. He was laying the foundation for a lifelong reading discipline, and he was enriching my language each time he'd sit down and ask me about those comic characters' lives.

In Summary: The Black Educational Challenge

Much of this writing has enunciated the challenges of educating Black young people in a racist society. I've described a historical and cultural framework for understanding the difficulty of raising our children to develop into community and race-conscious global citizens and critically thinking leaders. **Conscious awareness is the antecedent of any real change.** Indeed, there are strategies that can be deployed to ameliorate some of the pressing issues outlined in the previous pages. Some are simple, yet powerful strategies that only require awareness and deliberate action. Others will require actions from leaders across generations and professions. Traditional educators, policy strategists, youth development organizations, and media experts (as examples) are needed in this work; they must creatively and boldly pursue old and new pathways to radically transform the educational experience and outcomes for Black students.

PART II: GETTING TO QUALITY EDUCATION FOR BLACK CHILDREN, A REVOLUTIONARY ACT

113 |

Who Dropped the Ball on our Kids? Sondai K. Lester

"Black parents cannot trust the schools or streets to tell the children their story, or to do their job. Nor can black people expect an alien structure to have their, or their children's, best interests in mind."[43]

For those with a commitment to educating Black children, education cannot be viewed as though society has actually become post-racial or race neutral. To transcend the barriers to actualizing their full human potential, given the American system's determination to keep them in a second-class mentality, quality education for Black students must be viewed as a convergence of two themes: 1) mastering the skills to achieve and succeed in a global world, and 2) developing an unshakable positive sense of self-worth, not despite being Black, but because of it.

Hopefully, it's been established in the previous pages that as a social institution, the educational system's primary function has been and is the socialization of young people into an acceptance of the values and perspective of the dominant, power culture. Education has a *conserving* social role—to support and perpetuate

---

[43] Hare, Bruce and Lewis A. Castenell. No place to run, no place to hide! Comparative status and future prospects of black boys. In *Beginnings! The Social and Effective Development of Black Children*. (1985).

Who Dropped the Ball on our Kids? Sondai K. Lester

the historic power arrangement and social placement of groups. This conserving is carried out by overtly and covertly teaching the ideological foundation (albeit erroneous or built on a fabrication of history) upon which that reality was built and validated. The belief in the supremacy of whites and inferiority of people of color (especially Black people) is at the core.

The persistent failure of the educational system to prepare the masses of Black youth to function outside of the second-class, racially exploited status assigned to Black people is not a sign of the system's failure. It's an indication of its success.

Freedom in the world begins with freedom in the mind. When Black youth participate in an educational process that socializes them into a **counter-culture** with an affirming ideological foundation, they can then become psychologically able to resist and prevail against the racially-determined, second-class status waiting for them.

Considerations for those with a stake in educating Black children

The revolutionary educational process begins in the home—before children ever step foot in a school. The combined family, home and community life provides the child its *first* and essential exposure to an identity-affirming **counter-culture**. This culture fortifies the child to thrive and mitigate against the societally-imposed limitations with which he will certainly have to contend upon entering school.

To withstand and triumph in the face of the assault on Black identity, it is imperative that from childhood throughout adulthood Black youth and adults have ongoing exposure to counter-cultural affirming ideas and behaviors. These powerfully affirming reinforcers must come from all directions—home, school, artistic pursuits, church, sports leagues, extracurricular programs, and every area or institution that shapes the child's sense of self.

The counter-culture must extend outward—from the home into the community and then permeate the school environment. The counter-culture's powerful effect on the education of Black young people will show itself in such characteristics as community service, hard work, high expectations, racial solidarity, social responsibility, personal persistence, resilience in adversity, curiosity, self-regulation, effective self-expression and articulation, critical analysis, positive belief in self and others, etc.

Quality education for Black students requires a re-examination of the school curriculum and the environment of the home and community (as foundational places for education). The current "hidden curriculum" must be negated, even dismantled. In its place, a new and powerful foundation that builds within Black students self-efficacy, racial-esteem, and critical thinking competencies.

Parents, educators, teachers and community leaders must coalesce, strategize, collaborate and implement actions that build whole Black children. There are several areas to be considered in such an undertaking. Whether stakeholders take on small pieces or the whole endeavor, the key is to get started and remain focused—pick up the ball and run with it.

Several considerations require further exploration if we are to create a quality educational experience that builds new generations of Black leaders. This section introduces ideas related to a few of those areas. These and others require the commitment of many more to join the conscious educators who are already taking on these issues. What follows are seven questions that I wrestle with when considering Black young people within the context of 21st Century education in a global society. I also offer some starting responses and considerations.

Seven questions for teachers, parents, administrators and community agencies

1. What does it mean to adopt a liberating pedagogy?

2. What do we know about the nature of intelligence today, and why does it matter to Black students?

3. What should parents know and do to create a home environment (culture) that serves from birth onward as the foundation for their children's educational success?

4. How does education at home and school build the internal assets necessary for Black children to grow, navigate and thrive in the system of oppression?

5. How do schools and community agencies reintegrate the social and cultural educational components to build healthy racial identity and community collectivism?

6. Which curricular components are essential for academic success in the 21st Century global economy?

7. What *habits of mind* matter most for students in a global, technology-driven world?

QUESTION 1:
What does it mean to adopt a liberating pedagogy?

Educating our children from the inside out

The fundamental challenge to schooling a group of people that has been forced, then psychologically conditioned, to live in a

Who Dropped the Ball on our Kids? Sondai K. Lester

system that has oppressed and exploited them is to first **liberate them from that psychological enslavement.** It can't be overstated that the enslavement and subsequent oppression of Black people is a complex, protracted experience. It's one that imprisoned Blacks within a fabricated inferior identity and second-class status, and it has endured for over four centuries. The educational process must enable Black people to both identify and resist the social forces that create that inner bondage, while at the same time acquire the knowledge, skills and critical competencies for success in the contemporary, global society.

Unencumbered by psychic bondage, the oppressed can gain the freedom to use their education in service to liberating their group from powerlessness and dependency. Gaining psychological freedom, **because of their education** rather than despite it, allows the oppressed to go about the business of empowering their people. They recognize their responsibility to reach back to help make whole those mired in a state of chronic economic instability and hopelessness.

For Black students, **education from the inside out combines an affirming racial identity through the acquisition of knowledge of the real world with gaining essential competencies for personal success**. It fosters development of a constructive value system centered on social responsibility.

Within such an educational process, **the curricular framework should ensure that it:**

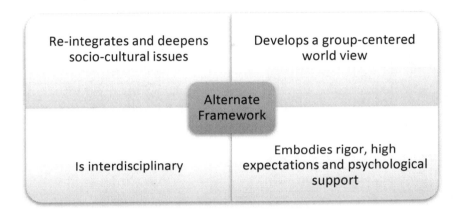

- Re-integrates and deepens the fundamental socio-cultural issues that permeate all learning areas.

- Develops students' view of the world that is grounded in the experiences of and implications for the oppressed, while simultaneously building acute awareness of how the system of oppression operates.

- Is inter-disciplinary, recognizing no content area exists in a vacuum. Education is transformative when its perspective is holistic—revealing how all content knowledge is a product of the ongoing interaction among disciplines.

- Embodies rigor and high expectations for achievement while providing the academic and psychological support to overcome negative racial environmental influences.

Who Dropped the Ball on our Kids? Sondai K. Lester

In a liberating educational paradigm, education, by necessity, derives from the inside out—from the students' historical, racial, social and cultural identity. It places the student at the center of the learning, and it recognizes that intelligence is not pre-determined by skin color.

> **In a liberating educational paradigm, education by necessity, derives from the inside out, from the students' historical, racial, social and cultural identity.**

Before looking at some of the suggested home and school curriculum considerations, a brief look at what is meant by intelligence might be helpful to parents and educators.

QUESTION 2
What do we know about the nature of intelligence today, and why does it matter to Black students?

We must rethink the meaning of "intelligence"

"Intelligence is the capacity to do something useful in the society in which we live. Intelligence is the ability to respond successfully to new situations and the capacity to learn from one's past experiences."[44] *Howard Gardner*

---

[44] Gardner, Howard (1993). *Multiple Intelligences: The Theory in Practice*

Who Dropped the Ball on our Kids? Sondai K. Lester

"IQ measures not just the quality of a person's mind but the quality of the world that person lives in."[45] Malcolm Gladwell

As Black people, we must overcome two myths about intelligence. The first is that Blacks and other groups of color are innately less endowed intellectually than whites. The second myth to overcome is that intelligence, once established and verified through IQ tests, is fixed for life. Neither erroneous assumption, however, should be disregarded because they are powerful influencers on how we parent and what we expect from education for our children. They must be addressed.

> **One's viewpoint about intelligence dramatically impacts the expectations for the level of achievement children can attain.**

There have been recent changing conceptions on the nature of intelligence, and they have profound implications on the process of raising children. One's viewpoint about intelligence dramatically impacts the expectations for the level of achievement children can attain and how parents go about pursuing their child's education. Up until the last 15 – 20 years, the prevailing notion had been that intelligence was determined by genetics and therefore immutable, i.e., fixed. The theory was that each child was born with a pre-established level of ability and potential for

---

[45] Gladwell, Malcolm (2008). *Outliers,* Little, Brown and Company

Who Dropped the Ball on our Kids? Sondai K. Lester

success that was passed down by its parents through their genes. Human outcomes consequently were viewed as a result of a fixed level of intelligence.

Genetically-determined, fixed intelligence was popularized by anthropologists during the 18th and 19th Centuries. Their theories served as scientific support of chattel slavery (the economic foundation for white American wealth). These "scholars" contrived and published a collection of theories purported to substantiate the intellectual and cultural preeminence of the white group. This allowed Europeans to reconcile in their minds the brutal treatment they imposed on Africans and the indigenous populations of the so-called "New World."

Then, in the early 20th Century, IQ tests were developed, based on the idea that intelligence was not only fixed at birth, but could be objectively measured. Tests were used to present data proving the biological superiority and inferiority of specific groups. These test results were accepted as valid measurements of intelligence without regard for the socio-economic impact on opportunity and the cognitive development experiences of groups scoring lower.

This idea of intelligence as static, rationalized by the prevailing scholarship of the time, inevitably was accepted by many of the Black and brown *victims* of this social caste system. It influenced the parenting practices in ways that unwittingly limited the level of expectation Black parents (and other excluded groups) had for

Who Dropped the Ball on our Kids? Sondai K. Lester

their children. These parents, through their negative social conditioning regarding race and education, set up a culture within their homes that would likely produce mediocre levels of achievement. This then served to further reinforce the societal assertion that Blacks are inherently intellectually inferior.

Given this pathological acceptance of their inferior intelligence, these parents' households tend to offer very limited cognitive engagement, challenge and expectation for academic outcomes. These households severely hinder children from developing the **habits of mind** that correlate with high intelligence. The children consequently score low on assessments of intelligence, perpetuating the cycle of low academic performance and transferring this negative identity to the next generation.

The school (along with the parents), by diminishing the level of cognitive challenge, demand, and expectation for the child, prepares the child to find and adapt to its place within the social caste system. Kozol speaks of two sets of school functions; the lesser of the two is the one for which many Black parents (although without awareness or deliberate intent) groom Black young people.

> *"But what is now encompassed by one word (school) are two very different kinds of institutions that, in function, finance, and intention, serve entirely different roles. Both are needed for our nation's governance. But children in one set of schools are educated to*

Who Dropped the Ball on our Kids? Sondai K. Lester

be governors; children in the other set of schools are trained to be governed." Jonathan Kozol, Savage Inequalities (1991)

The child, not knowing any better, compliantly goes along with this self-destructive process. They are, in reality, primed by their home and school environment to achieve far below their potential as the "less than" messages and reinforcements over time become irresistible forces.

Malcolm Gladwell in his book *Blink*[46] draws the following conclusion:

> *"As a society, we place enormous faith in tests because we think that they are a reliable indicator of the test taker's ability and knowledge. But are they really? If a white student from a prestigious private high school gets a higher SAT score than a black student from an inner-city school, is it because she's truly a better student, or is it because to be white and to attend a prestigious high school is to be constantly **primed** with the idea of smart?" p. 57*

Human intelligence is dynamic, not static. Intelligence is not an entity fixed and determined at birth by genetic factors. In 1984, social scientist James Flynn[47] discovered that human intelligence across the world had been rising every decade since intelligence

---

[46] Gladwell, Malcolm (2005). *Blink: The Power of Thinking Without Thinking*
[47] Flynn, James R. The mean IQ of Americans: Massive gains 1932 to 1978. *Psychological Bulletin.* 1984, 95: 29–51

Who Dropped the Ball on our Kids? Sondai K. Lester

tests had first been administered. His findings demonstrated that with each succeeding generation, IQ scores have risen. The reasons are not fully explained, though Flynn believes the phenomenon is related to environmental influences. Flynn's observations ran counter to the notion that intelligence was

> **Individual intelligence can be raised throughout life and along with it the abilities and capacity of the individual to function in the world.**

permanently fixed. We now understand that intelligence is continually cultivated and mediated by both internal and external forces. The simple graphic that follows, based on Flynn and others' work, is good news for those who've believed there's little they can do to raise intelligent children; IQ has risen and continues to rise over time.

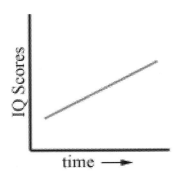

Individual intelligence can be raised throughout life and along with it the abilities and capacity of the individual to thrive and achieve at increasingly higher levels.

Who Dropped the Ball on our Kids? Sondai K. Lester

Over the last two decades researchers have developed more specific definitions of the nature and complexity of human intelligence. These definitions have not only clarified the complex essence of intelligence and its variety of expressions but also the crucial role that environment plays in its development and expansion. In this evolving and alternate view of the concept of intelligence, clearly traditional methods for assessing individual intelligence are inadequate.

The current and narrow forms of assessing intelligence on standardized tests unfairly and incorrectly categorize large numbers of Black children as having below average intelligence. This implies then that Black children have less capability and potential than others who score higher on these assessments. The results of these assessments almost always have an adverse impact on the beliefs that parents, teachers, and the children themselves have about their capacity to achieve at high academic levels.

Belief affects actions. Parents, teachers and children become imprisoned by the false notion that these standardized assessments of intelligence reflect a permanent inability to perform or compete at high academic levels. Lowered expectations and diminished motivation are inevitabilities given the self-negating power of these test scores on families of color. This reduced motivation and energy produces outcomes on a spectrum between dismal to average, then sets in motion a vicious downward confidence spiral, intensifying the belief in the race's limited intellectual capacity.

Extending the definition: Three views of intelligence

Three notable authors' scholarship in this effort to redefine the nature and development of intelligence include **Howard Gardner, Robert Sternberg, and Daniel Goleman**. Howard Gardner, a psychology professor at Harvard University, contends that the traditional form of IQ testing is far too limited. His research points to the idea of **multiple intelligences**. He posits that there are eight different intelligences that reflect the broad range of potential existing in humans. Since most IQ tests or ability assessments are limited to two areas, linguistic and mathematics, they can be punitive for children whose intellectual strengths lie in other of the six intelligences.

Some parents and educators become aware of children's gifts (intelligences) beyond language and math as they observe and interact with them. Often even when these other intelligences are observed, they are not cultivated for fear that they might not be the ones society will reward later with lucrative roles in the workplace. However, given the dynamism of the modern world, many of these intelligences have proven to be differentiators for innovation and creatively solving significant challenges in today's and tomorrow's world.

Gardner's Eight Multiple Intelligences[48]

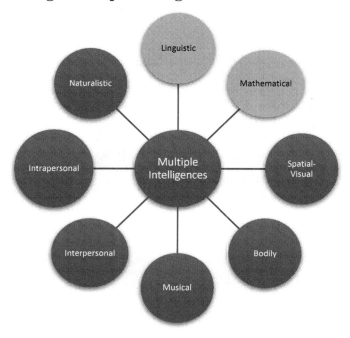

- *Linguistic intelligence (word smart)*
- *Logical-Mathematical intelligence (number/reasoning smart)*
- *Spatial-Visual intelligence (position smart)*
- *Bodily-Kinesthetic intelligence (body-movement smart)*
- *Musical intelligence (music smart)*
- *Inter-personal intelligence (people smart)*
- *Intra-personal intelligence (self-smart)*
- *Naturalistic intelligence (nature/science smart)*

To what extent are you as teacher or parent aware of the dominant, natural intelligences of your children? Are they extraordinarily inclined towards

---

[48] Gardner, Howard (1983). *Frames of Mind: The Theory of Multiple Intelligences*

Who Dropped the Ball on our Kids? Sondai K. Lester

people smarts (interpersonal)? Are they drawn towards nature, or things that require physicality (bodily) or are they deeply reflective (intrapersonal)? To prepare them to soar in areas that extend out from their unique drives requires paying attention.

The second of the three theories mentioned related to taking a broader view of intelligence is **Successful Intelligence**. It was put forth by Dr. Robert Sternberg, professor from Cornell University. The theory states that the traditional standardized tests measuring only an individual's ability in analytic reasoning in core academic subjects is not sufficient to predict future success in a career as an adult. Sternberg defines three areas of intelligence. When compared with Gardner's, some similarities are apparent. Sternberg's represent a number of Gardner's more succinctly, with the clustering into three. Together these three make up *successful intelligence* and provide another basis to predict meaningful outcomes for children in adulthood.

Three Successful Intelligence components:

- *Academic intelligence – analytic reasoning*
- *Personal intelligence – knowledge of self and others*
- *Practical intelligence – environmental adaptation and dealing with the give and take of daily life*

Then, a third examination of what constitutes intelligence, worthy of our consideration, comes from Rutgers professor Dr. Daniel Goleman. He developed what's now a familiar yet woefully

Who Dropped the Ball on our Kids? Sondai K. Lester

underdeveloped intelligence in American society, **emotional intelligence** (referred to as **EQ**). Dr. Goleman's research led him to the conclusion that it is not the narrow traditional models of IQ that determine human intelligence and success as an adult. A large portion of one's success as an adult is based on EQ. One's EQ is an intelligence that is cultivated based on the kind of behaviors and relationships established between the individual and the significant others within one's environment.

Goleman's four domains of emotional intelligence (EQ)

- ***Self-awareness*** - *the ability to read your emotions and recognize their impact on others*

- ***Self-management*** – *involves controlling/regulating one's emotions and impulses and adapting to changing circumstances*

- **Social awareness** – *the ability to sense, understand, and react to the emotions of others, while comprehending the dynamics of the current social networks*

- **Relationship management** – *the ability to inspire, influence, and develop others while effectively managing conflict*

The message then, related to Question 2, is that it's imperative that parents and other stakeholders know there's an evolving view of intelligence. Intelligence can constantly grow, and there are things that can be done to foster that growth. These three expansive views of intelligence (noted above) should remind child development stakeholders and parents that they have both an opportunity and responsibility to act in ways that enable Black children to actualize their many potentialities.

QUESTION 3

What should parents know and do to create a home environment (culture) that serves from birth onward as the foundation for their children's educational success?

Home and school factors for expanding intelligence

All three of these views (multiple intelligences, success intelligence and emotional intelligence) assert that intelligence isn't fixed; it's malleable. In addition, they indicate that the growth and expansion of intelligence require attending to both internal and external factors. All these factors are continually being influenced, for better or worse, by the actions of the significant adults in a

Who Dropped the Ball on our Kids? Sondai K. Lester

child's life beginning with the parents. For the child's first five years, the parents have primary control over the environmental

> **It is the parents' responsibility to learn the factors that create a *counter-priming process* and then put them in place during the child's early development.**

factors (internal and external) that are key to developing the child's intelligence. It is the parents' duty to override the dominant societal frame of mind and **prime** their children to feel and behave in *smart ways*.

Parents often do not realize that even in the face of tremendous societal inequities, children can prevail and overcome them when their parents have built a "smart" success-cultivating home environment. In it, they acquire the foundational capacities and will to survive and thrive despite external pressure for low expectations. The home, critically important for children in under-resourced, urban Black and brown communities, is as important to a child's resilience and success as are the social structures outside of the home.

Parents then, would be wise to learn the factors to create a counter-priming process and then put these factors in place beginning with the child's early, critical development. Parents have tremendous power; they lay the foundation for their children to engage in a lifelong process of enriching and expanding their intelligence. How do they actualize this parent power? They do it by providing the child with the skills and knowledge to become happy, productive, and successful. They do it by maintaining an acute awareness that **the environment can expand intelligence**. They do it by investing themselves in creating a growth-enhancing environment. These actions can yield significant positive results.

What follows are some of the internal and external factors that influence the development of intelligence. Parents and educators should be aware of these, then mold their mindsets around them as they support Black children with maximizing their potential.

Internal factors influencing intelligence. These are some of the factors internal to the parents and the young child that either hinder or help the quality of the child's future academic trajectory.

- Genetic inheritance
- Mother's pre-natal nutrition practices
- Mother's pre-natal psycho-emotional state
- Mental habits

- Pre-natal relationship between mother and father (state of mind)
- Post-natal density of neural wiring
- Child's attitude and beliefs about self

Six of the seven factors above are directly controllable by the parents. Genetics are inherited; and, while that can't be changed, parents can work, for example, to build healthy relationships and state of mind for both themselves and their offspring. The density of neural wiring can be influenced by the experience the child has within the household. For example, exposing young children to more complex sounds and language automatically forces the brain to work harder and thereby enhances the child's neural wiring.

External, societal factors influencing intelligence

Many of the following external factors can be positively influenced by parents and other adults in a child's life, overriding the tendency for these factors to show up as deficiencies.

Category	*Influence*
Health	• Pre-natal medical monitoring • Post-natal medical monitoring
Home	• *Parenting style* • *Type of parental communication with children* • *Engagement and exposure that stimulates child's brain development* • *Home routine and structure that sets level of expectations for achievement* • *Parental relationships (level of involvement of both parents)* • *Resources (amount, variety and complexity)* • *Defined boundaries and outcomes for behavior and performance* • *Extent and quality of involvement in child's educational process (in and outside of school)* • *Adult/parental extent of personal involvement in lifelong learning*

Who Dropped the Ball on our Kids? Sondai K. Lester

School	• Resources (amount and variety)
	• Curriculum's effect on students' survival skills and habits of mind (See Wagner and Costa in next section)
	• Curriculum effect on development of emotional intelligence as a literacy
	• Pedagogy based on contemporary "digital native" learning style; technology engagement is fundamental
	• Curriculum and its cultural relevance
	• Parental involvement structures, quality and promotion
	• Staff development emphasis and frequency
	• Community resources, engagement, service learning and related "real" issues incorporated into the educational process
	• Opportunities to cultivate a range of intelligences, beyond language and mathematics
Exposure	• Amount and type of travel
	• Range of diverse cultural activities
	• Extent of engagement in extra-curricular activities
	• Involvement in other learning institutions (e.g., museums, galleries, college campuses, libraries, etc.)
	• Involvement in volunteerism and service projects

What you can do to expand intelligence

Parents who are committed to raising high-achieving children make deliberate efforts to establish an asset rich (nurturing and challenging) home environment early in their children's lives. They consider and invest in both the internal and external influences they can have on their children's development. (Investing in these doesn't always require money; time, attention, and choice are invaluable resources to invest.) Intentional parenting shows itself when parents adopt healthy communication and other patterns that are common to households of high achieving students. They adopt specific habits and behaviors that have proven to be differentiators between high achieving Black students and their lower-achieving peers. These practices have allowed children to succeed despite the socio-economic and curricular obstacles. University of Chicago economists James J. Heckman and Dimitriy V. Masterov said[49]:

> *"Successful schools build on the efforts of successful families. The family is a major producer of the skills and motivation required for producing successful students in schools and workers in the market. Both cognitive and non-cognitive abilities are shaped early in the life cycle and differences in abilities persist."*

Some suggested actions are based on two comprehensive qualitative studies conducted by Reginald M. Clark[50] and William A. Sampson.[51] These activities, relationships and attitudes establish a home culture for raising children to act in *smart ways*. Clark's basic position is that **the family's main contribution to a child's success in school is made through parents' dispositions and interpersonal relationships with their**

---

[49] The productivity argument for investing in young children. *Review of Agricultural Economics*, 29:3 p. 446-493.

[50] Clark, R. M. (1983). *Family Life and School Achievement: Why Poor Black Children Succeed or Fail*

[51] Sampson, W. A. (2004). *Black and Brown: Race, Ethnicity, and School Preparation*

children in the household. Clark says that children receive essential "survival knowledge" for competent classroom behavior from their exposure to positive home attitudes and positive patterns of communication.

These home patterns among high achieving students have the following characteristics:

- Large amounts of **parent involvement and interest** in children's home activities
- Consistent parental monitoring of children's **use of time and space**
- Frequent, almost ritualistic, **parent and child activities involving studying,** reading, writing, conversing, and creating
- Regular parental explanation, advisement, and demonstration of **everyday life skills** to the child
- Consistent parental **expectation and standards** for responsible and restricted child behavior
- Parents **never questioning** their children's innate self-worth or ability to achieve at high levels
- Regular **praiseworthy sentiments** expressed for the child's talents, abilities, and achievements (a higher ratio of encouragements over discouragements)
- Consistently challenging children to **think critically** and creatively

- Parents constantly **expressing their love** for their children in words and behavior

- Parents approach discipline from an **authoritative** perspective (using reasoning and giving room for children to make decisions and learn from mistakes) rather than **authoritarian** (with very little involvement, parental teaching, advising, or sharing of concepts and ideas; giving frequent criticism and attacks on child's self-worth)

- Parents **model disciplined parenting** behavior

Sampson's key question related to closing the racial achievement gap is: *Why, given the same demographic factors, do some Black youth from working class or poverty level have households that raise children who are academically successful while so many others do not?* Sampson identified some family household indicators that lay the foundation for positive academic outcomes for children, which are similar to Clark's findings:

- **High expectations** – parents believe in their children's innate capacity to achieve at high academic levels and hold them accountable for attaining those outcomes

- **Discipline** is reinforced within the household – parents maintain and affirm a certain acceptable standard of behavior, role boundaries, and basic responsibility for the functioning of the household

Who Dropped the Ball on our Kids? Sondai K. Lester

- **Delayed gratification** is emphasized (simple immediate rewards are discouraged while more meaningful delayed rewards are encouraged), and tasks and discipline necessary for success are prioritized

- Involvement in and **monitoring of schoolwork** daily along with consistent interaction with the administrative and teaching staff of the school

- **Modeling the importance of learning** – parents read newspapers, books and magazines (print and online), keep informed about and discuss current events in the house; parents are engaged in a personal process of self-improvement and continuous learning

- **Civic participation** – consistent voter and community volunteerism

Be deliberate about the messages you want the family/home culture to send to your children. Ask yourself questions like these:

- What messages do I want my child to get from his or her home environment?

- What in the household supports the messaging I desire?

- What in the household currently contradicts or undermines the messaging?

- What actions can I take, or what behaviors can I (or we) demonstrate to enhance the family's culture and its messages?

Who Dropped the Ball on our Kids? Sondai K. Lester

During a recent visit to a nearby elementary school, I was pleased to see colorful, well designed messages displayed so children (and parents) can see them as they enter the school and walk the hallways. There were many statements, including: *I am limitless. I am a creator. I am a good listener. I am curious. I am a risk taker.* Other similar visual and implicit messages in the home might include: *I can learn anything when I make the effort. I am fully capable. I can figure it out. I have ideas to contribute. I work hard to achieve my goals. Problems are opportunities to stretch my thinking. I am valuable to my community. I give and deserve respect.*

QUESTION 4

How does education at home and school build the internal assets necessary to succeed, grow, navigate and thrive in the system of oppression?

Home/School: Fostering an asset-rich environment

In support of the suggestions on optimizing the home environment, those with a stake in educating Black children might find it instructive to look at the work on creating an asset-rich environment for children. One such framework is the Search Institute's **40 Developmental Assets**[52]. (There are other frameworks worth exploring that are more succinct.) A sampling of eight items from the 40 Assets that help establish a positive,

---

[52] Search-institute.org

strengths-based environment for raising strong resilient children are listed here:

- **Other Adult Relationships** (children receive ongoing support from three or more nonparent adults)
- **Caring neighborhood** (children experience caring neighbors)
- **Safety** (children feel safe at home, school and in their neighborhood)
- **Positive Peer Influence** (children have best friends who model responsible behavior)
- **Resistance Skills** (youth can resist negative peer pressure and dangerous situations)
- **Personal Power** (young person feels he or she has control over what happens to them)
- **Sense of Purpose** (young person believes his or her life has a purpose)
- **Reading for Pleasure** (young person reads for pleasure three or more hours weekly)

How can you ensure that these factors are in place in the home and neighborhood? Which factors need your attention? Which are already in place? Environment matters when raising children. It's even more crucial for Black children who have to function in and fight against an institutional context that has decided Black people are inferior.

Who Dropped the Ball on our Kids? Sondai K. Lester

Cultivate a growth mindset: It matters

Black young people cannot break free from a negative life trajectory unless they adopt a mindset with messages that counter the disaffirming mindset society imposes. Carol Dweck's[53] groundbreaking work around two types of mindsets and the impact on human learning and success examines the effect of mindset on students. Dweck describes mindset as *a perception or theory people hold about themselves.* For example, if a Black child is raised to believe he is smart (and behaves accordingly), that's a mindset; conversely if she is constantly told she is not very bright, that fosters a mindset too. Mindset affects how people approach all aspects of their lives, whether people are consciously aware of their mindset or not. Mindset work is growing in popularity for children and adults because it can either be debilitating or enhancing—with potentially lifelong effects.

Dweck identifies two mindsets: **fixed and growth**. Fixed is the most limiting type of mindset. She describes a **fixed mindset** as:

> *"People believe their basic qualities, like their intelligence or talent, are simply fixed traits. They spend their time documenting their intelligence or talent instead of developing them."*

Those with a fixed mindset believe either you have it, or you don't. They fail to recognize the power of putting forth effort and

---

[53] Dweck, Carol (2006). *Mindset: The New Psychology of Success*

making multiple attempts at achieving goals. In the case of African American students, society leads them to believe that their race is the cause of and symbol for their fixed and inescapable lower intelligence when compared to whites. The school's hidden curriculum and its tracking system reinforce and perpetuate this racially-based, negative fixed mindset.

Fixed mindsets can affect children whether they are told they are smart or dumb. Too often, Black children develop a "I'm dumb" mindset. On the other hand, to lessen the effects of societal conditioning to accept a personally-negating belief system, some Black parents habitually tell their children how naturally brilliant they are ("naturally brilliant" also reflects a fixed mindset). This can be to their detriment because these young people often falter when they meet a challenge that is not easily solved. They fear failure and have not been taught the reward of hard work, of ongoing effort. How many of us tell our children how naturally brilliant they are? "Be careful" would be the advice of those doing mindset work, as the children can end up with weak resilience skills in the face of challenge or adversity.

Alternately, with a **growth mindset**, according to Dweck,

> *"People believe that their most basic abilities can be developed through dedication and hard work—brains and talent are just the starting point. This view creates a love of learning and a resilience that is essential for great accomplishment."*

Who Dropped the Ball on our Kids? Sondai K. Lester

When children have the mindset that they can learn, that they can become smarter, the research indicates they don't worry much about failure or challenge. In fact, they embrace these as ways to learn more and learn faster than those whose mindsets are fixed.

For Black children, with all the social pressure to believe they are "fixed" in an inferior status because of their race, it's imperative for parents and educators to nurture a growth mindset. The child must be raised to deeply internalize that all human realities, including individual intelligence and accomplishment are malleable and can be altered through their own actions. Shifting mindsets may feel like swimming upstream, but it must be done and has been done with great success.

There is power in rewarding effort and rigor as much as results. Dweck's work meshes well with one of Malcolm Gladwell's ideas expressed in his best-selling book Outliers.[54] He shares that most often it's not innate, fixed talent but discipline, practice, effort and constantly pushing at the boundaries of what we know that enables achieving greatness. Says Gladwell (p. 246):

> *"Success is a function of persistence and doggedness and the willingness to work hard for twenty-two minutes to make sense of something that most people would give up on after thirty seconds."*

---

[54] Gladwell, Malcolm (2008). *Outliers: The Story of Success*

Who Dropped the Ball on our Kids? Sondai K. Lester

For parents, this means continually reinforcing with their children that intelligence is expanded through their hard work and cannot be defined solely through objective tests or the color of their skin. **Children ought to be encouraged to value the learning process**—the journey towards knowledge and insight and not just the grade the child receives on a test. Children must be raised to know that learning is an opportunity for self-improvement and expansion of their thinking capability. In this context, failure is an opportunity to more closely analyze the process of problem-solving rather than a symbol of one's personal inadequacy.

The common habit of chasing grades or choosing subjects easily grasped sometimes shows itself among "smart" Black students who've matriculated through middle and high school without much effort. They didn't discern that low expectations are built into most urban school curricula. So, when these "smart" students move into a setting with higher expectations, often university settings with majority white students or when taking mandatory college entry exams, they often freeze and begin to feel inadequate. They have not developed the discipline of study nor the confidence to challenge the boundaries of their current knowledge. They didn't realize the more complex the subject, the more rigor and hard work are required to master the content. It doesn't mean the student is incapable when he or she doesn't immediately solve a complex problem. It only appears so because educators and parents assumed good grades at a low-expectations

Who Dropped the Ball on our Kids? Sondai K. Lester

school meant they were naturally brilliant. The students had not been prepared for behavioral discipline and rigorous thinking.

The development of a growth mindset requires parents practice giving their children more pats on the back and acknowledgement for their **effort** rather than accolades for getting the **right answer**. *So, pay attention to what you are rewarding.* Reward process. Reward discipline. Reward thinking. Reward resilience. Shift away from telling the child that he or she is the smartest, the cutest, or the best when they've demonstrated little rigor, and avoided the challenges necessary to grow.

Why reward effort and resilience? Because these lead to practices that bolster the child's competence and confidence to learn and ultimately lead to better outcomes. Says Dweck in her November 2014 TED Talk, *The Power of Believing That You Can Improve*:

> *"We can praise wisely, not praising intelligence or talent. That has failed. Don't do that anymore. But praising the process that kids engage in: their effort, their strategies, their focus, their perseverance, their improvement. This process praise creates children who are hardy and resilient."*

It can't be overstated: One of the most important things parents can do is to help their children develop the character traits to not only build a growth mindset but also sustain it to engage in an ongoing process of learning. Some of these character traits for building a growth mindset include:

- Persistence and resilience in the face of obstacles and mistakes
- Curiosity and creativity
- Optimism concerning their personal capacity to succeed
- Conscientiousness towards responsibilities
- Openness, honesty and compassion in their relationships
- Emotional self-regulation
- Willingness to work collaboratively to find answers
- Openness to diversity of people and ideas

The work parents have to do in the home to foster a growth mindset within their children goes hand-in-hand with exposing them to Black people's historical accomplishments of civilization-creation and development. These significant achievements are evidence of the power of a growth mindset among Black people. Grounding Black children in the knowledge that they are part of a group that built ancient great nations as well as persevered through times of great pain including physical slavery strengthens them for life today. The barrier-breaking achievements of Black scholars, scientists, artists, and athletes are clear indicators that skills and intelligence can and do grow. Psychologists, including

Who Dropped the Ball on our Kids? Sondai K. Lester

Marilynn Brewer and Wendi Gardner[55], have determined that when individuals feel they are a part of a high-performing group, they are personally motivated to achieve at high levels, and they have a heightened sense of obligation to solving group problems.

QUESTION 5
How do schools and community agencies reintegrate the social and cultural educational components to build healthy racial identity and community collectivism?

Attending to Black children's social and cultural development

Reconsidering the social and cultural context is more than restoring relics of the African and African-American past. Self-understanding, racial pride, an ability to analyze the historical context and tragic experiences endured by one's people, exploring the culture and history of other non-white groups are key to developing a healthy foundation for a young person. These provide a sense of placement and continuity.

Integrating or even grounding a Black child's education from an African centered perspective is as important or more important than the technical skill-building for success as an adult. This

---

[55] Brewer, Marilynn and Gardner, Wendi. Who is this "We"? Levels of collective identity and self-representations. *Journal of Personality and Social Psychology. Vol. 71:1, p. 83-93. 1996.*

perspective can bring forth a lasting affirming effect on self-identification as parents cultivate whole, powerful Black children.

An excerpt from Detroit Public Schools' African-Centered Education strands begins by saying that African Centered Education is "based on research indicating all humans have their physical, social, and intellectual origins in Africa." This is both powerful and historically accurate, yet largely unknown by Black people. From pre-K through Grade 3, the social studies curriculum established in 1994[56] was summarized as follows:

Social Studies Scope and Sequence	African Centered Education Outcomes and Objectives
PK-K: Myself and Others	Develop a positive self-concept, emphasizing values, ethnic background and culture as reflected in the principles of unity, self-determination, collective work and responsibility, cooperative economics, purpose, creativity and faith (Nguzo Saba) • Identify self • Recognize the importance of one's name to one's identity • Define a family and name ways in which different families celebrate different holidays
Grade 1: School and Family	Develop a positive concept about family, emphasizing self-worth, values, ethnic background and culture as reflected in the principles of unity, self-determination, collective work and responsibility, cooperative economics, purpose, creativity and faith (Nguzo Saba)

---

[56] Social Studies Core Curriculum Outcomes and Objectives: Pre-Kindergarten – Grade 12 Curriculum Document. Prepared by the Office of Social Studies, Detroit Public Schools, June 1994.

	• Describe the importance of family as a basic unit of society • Identify examples of positive concepts involving families • Compare and contrast the family unit in Africa and America
Grade 2: **Neighborhood**	Develop a positive concept about neighborhood, emphasizing self-worth, values, ethnic background and culture reflected in the principles of unity, self-determination, collective work and responsibility, cooperative economics, purpose, creativity and faith (Nguzo Saba) • Compare and contrast the concept of village life in Africa with the concept of neighborhoods in the United States
Grade 3: **Communities/Detroit**	Understand the importance of cultural transmission. • Identify elements in African American culture retained from African origins • Describe ways in which folktales, music, dance, and art define the culture • Describe and analyze Paradise Valley (Detroit) or other historic Black areas in the city as a model of a culture community within an urban environment

What we see here is that a young person starts early connecting learning and life to a historically accurate origin in Africa. Whether the student is Black or white, it begins with historical correctness. Black students were expected to examine their own lives, families and communities within the larger context of their African origins.

Who Dropped the Ball on our Kids? Sondai K. Lester

Every Black child should be well versed, from a historical perspective, in the following defining events and epochs. They should also be exposed to Black literature as well as be supported in developing an informed point of view and analytic framework to interpret current affairs.

Social studies, themes in history

- In the beginning-Gondwanaland
- African origins of civilization
- African discovery of the "New World"
- Politics and economics of the African slave trade (Christianity and Islam)
- The making of a slave—seasoning in the Caribbean islands and "the mark of oppression"
- Colonial era (in the Americas and Africa)
- Spirit of resistance to slavery
- Civil War: Politics, race and economics
- Reconstruction and Black progress
- Post-Reconstruction, Jim Crow and stamping out Black progress
- Northern migration
- Civil Rights and Black Power movements
- African freedom struggles
- Neo-colonialism

Literature: Intensive exploration of these defining Black cultural revolutionary themes:

- Ante-bellum South
- Post-bellum South
- Harlem Renaissance
- Civil Rights and Black Power

Who Dropped the Ball on our Kids? Sondai K. Lester

- Post-Civil Rights
- Pre- & Post-Colonial Africa and the Caribbean

Contemporary Affairs

- Post industrialism and the emergence of a global economy
- Institutionalized racism— "Two Nations" (based on race and class)
- Myth of post-racialism (The new Jim Crow—income inequality and gentrification)
- Social and media processes in building a psychology of racial inferiority— "The Black Image in the White Mind" (Robert Entman and Andrew Rojecki, 2001)

QUESTION 6

Which curricular components are essential for academic success in the 21st Century global economy?

21st Century education: A curricular starting point

Besides the social-cultural development of Black children, academic success in a 21st Century global society should consider a number of requisite subjects. The transition (beginning in the latter third of the 20th Century) from an industrial, labor-intensive, production economy to a post-industrial, technology-fueled economy dramatically altered the competencies required for economic success. The first, with reliance on low-skilled workers, was then supplanted by the modern workplace requiring an educated, service-oriented workforce. Industrial era educational outcomes were tied to knowing and reproducing the single "correct"

Who Dropped the Ball on our Kids? Sondai K. Lester

answer—the one the teacher required. Obedience to authority, memory and rote recall of content were the primary competencies necessary for school success.

Educational outcomes for the 21st Century are quite different. They are centered around solving problems that may have no prescribed answers, problems for which even the teacher may not have an answer. The focus in this new learning milieu is on production of knowledge, rather than rigid reproduction of information.

Modern technology has accelerated the rate at which an individual's accumulated knowledge accrues. What once may have taken decades or a lifetime to learn can now be acquired in years and even months. Since our existence is driven by the inevitability and irresistibility of change, the question becomes: *How do we build students' capability to function intelligently in the face of the rapidity of change and the expansion of knowledge?* Those who have not been imprisoned by and limited to the current level of accumulated knowledge can evolve their thinking. They can not only comprehend the emerging thinking but also produce new ways of understanding existence. Those with the competencies to participate intelligently in this new era are at a decided advantage over those trapped in the old ideas, many of which are no longer effective in the new order.

Parents, as they select schools, can inquire about the six broad topics below to determine whether and to what extent they will need to augment their children's education.

1.Science, Technology, Engineering and Mathematics (STEM)

2. Foreign Language:

- Mastery of at least one foreign language
- Involvement with native-speakers of that language

3. Arts: Instrumental, vocal, theater, painting, sculpture, broadcast, dance, writing: Essays, plays, poetry, short stories

4. Community Service: Ongoing service projects (visioning, planning, executing and evaluating community impact)

5. Sports: Opportunity to engage in at least one sport as a support for learning teamwork, physical coordination, discipline and strategic thinking

6. Business Administration: Entrepreneurship, marketing, accounting, product design, e-commerce, business plans, management

---

QUESTION 7
What "habits of mind" matter most for students in a global, technology-driven world?

21st Century habits of mind and survival skills

"When we no longer know what to do we have come to our real work, and when we no longer know which way to go we have begun our real journey. The mind that is not baffled is not employed. The impeded stream is the one that sings." Wendell Berry

Developing 21st Century competencies and knowledge of social and racial realities ought to be embedded in the curriculum and pedagogy of today's teachers. These aptitudes are in effect the processes and strategies students will continually utilize to

Who Dropped the Ball on our Kids? Sondai K. Lester

effectively master all content areas. Albert Costa[57] refers to these as *habits of mind*. Some of these habits overlap and amplify the *seven survival skills* articulated by Tony Wagner[58]. These capabilities, explicated by others in varying ways, provide the student-as-learner the tools to function intelligently in our contemporary society. Wagner's *seven survival skills* for educators' consideration are:

1. Critical thinking and problem-solving
2. Collaboration across networks and leading with influence
3. Agility and adaptability
4. Initiative and entrepreneurialism
5. Effective oral and written communication
6. Accessing and analyzing information
7. Curiosity and imagination

[57] Costa, Albert and Kallick, Bena (2009). *Habits of Mind Across the Curriculum: Practical and Creative Strategies for Teachers*
[58] Wagner, Tony (2008). *The Global Achievement Gap: Why Even Our Best Schools Don't Teach the New Survival Skills Our Children Need—And What to Do About It,* Basic Books.

Both parents and teachers can ask themselves: *How does or can our home (or for teachers, our classroom) help build rigor and muscle in these seven skill areas? What is working now? What else can be built into these important learning environments? What activities can we do to enhance these capacities?* **(See the worksheet with activities and reflections on page 164 as a starting point.)**

Costa's sixteen *habits of mind*, which, as indicated, subsume some of Wagner's seven survival skills. They are identified below and could be converted into a checklist for teachers, parents or students to make a non-threatening assessment to determine what each of these stakeholders needs to do to develop these habits among students.

☐ **Critical thinking and problem solving**—the exercise of sound reasoning and analytical techniques to systematically work through facts and data to solve real life problems

☐ **Listening with understanding and empathy**—the capacity to detect and accept the feelings and points of view of others even when they conflict with your own

Listening is the beginning of understanding. Wisdom is the reward for a lifetime of listening. Let the wise listen and add to their learning and let the discerning get guidance. Proverbs 1:5

☐ **Oral communication**—the ability to articulate thoughts and ideas clearly and effectively to others

☐ **Written communication**—the ability to critically explore a problem or issue and write reports and research results clearly and logically

Who Dropped the Ball on our Kids? Sondai K. Lester

- Teamwork/collaboration—the ability to build collaborative relationships with peers and effectively work in diverse teams with the capacity to negotiate and manage conflicts in ways that maintain the integrity and viability of the team

- Information and technological literacy—the ability to select and utilize the appropriate technology to successfully accomplish a task or solve the identified problem

- Leadership—the ability to leverage the unique skills of others to accomplish a common goal; to use interpersonal skills to influence others towards actions that bring about their personal growth; an openness to new ideas and learning from others

- Managing impulsivity—the ability to think before one acts; to intentionally establish a vision of a product, an action plan, a goal and delay immediate gratification in order to systematically act towards completion of the plan or goal

- Questioning and posing problems—the capacity to clearly identify a problem by asking probing questions to fill in the gaps between what you know and what you don't know.

"The formulation of a problem is often more essential than its solution. To raise new questions, new possibilities, regarding old problems from a new angle, requires creative imagination and marks real advances." Albert Einstein

- Taking responsible risks—a willingness to try something new and different, accepting the fact that you will probably make mistakes

☐ **Thinking about your own thinking (metacognition)**—being aware of your own thoughts, feelings and intentions with a recognition of how what you do impacts others; to explore "Why do I think the way I do about this?"

☐ **Diversity and inclusion**—the capacity to learn from and work collaboratively with individuals representing other cultures, neighborhoods, races, gender, religions, lifestyles, and points of view on common problems

☐ **Creativity/innovation**—to demonstrate originality and inventiveness in work (always seeking the next level in concept or design), to communicate new ideas to others, to integrate knowledge across disciplines

☐ **Lifelong learning/self-direction**—continuously seeking to acquire new knowledge and skills, continually analyzing one's growth needs with the ability to accept and learn from personal mistakes

☐ **Ethics and social responsibility**—engaging others with respect and integrity, keeping the interests and needs of the larger group as primary

☐ **Professionalism**—demanding personal accountability from self and others reflected in a disciplined committed approach to the work involved in successfully completing the tasks taken on by the individual and groups to which the individual belongs

These are beginning responses to the seven questions I posed based on experience and research. They will require parents, teachers, educational administrators, policy makers, community leaders and

Who Dropped the Ball on our Kids? Sondai K. Lester

the students themselves to seek and act on coherent, creative answers and relevant strategies. Strategies must fit the times.

Our propensity to hold on to tactics, strategies and concepts for revolutionary activity 50 years ago must be balanced with the reality of contemporary changes and required skills to function and lead in a global, technological world. Historical Black movements have stagnated around well-worn approaches and are hopefully entering a period of Wendell's "bafflement"—thinking of new approaches to the increasing complexity of liberating Black people in a fast-paced, connected, technological global society. What does it even mean today to "liberate" Black people? From what? Where? Who are we talking about? And how do we get there? What's for sure is that as educators, the changing world requires expanding the skill and socio-cultural repertoire of today's and tomorrow's Black students as leaders.

Concluding Remarks to Parents and Educators: The Ball is in Your Court

As Kenny, Ira and I continue reflecting on our educational leadership journey, we are still studying, making efforts, providing support and mentoring to make a difference at this juncture in our lives. It's lifelong work, carried out in different ways at different stages. We are not certain whether our winding paths amount to dropping the ball or just holding it static during the more complex decades and rapid change. What we do know is that we care deeply and remain committed to transforming the lives of Black people and our communities, especially through the education of our young people. We hold firm that affecting their minds and aspirations is critical to elevating and liberating Black people.

So, to you, our current education leaders and parents-as-teachers, your time is now.

The process of education, to be relevant for marginalized groups, must seriously consider the political ramifications of its curriculum. Be reminded: Curriculum is developed to maintain the social hierarchy and power positions of the dominant group (in this case the white privileged group) at the expense of all others. As educators, you can help mitigate against this reality by reflecting on and implementing strategies to create, augment or find an educational process that builds a healthy racial identity among African American young people. Alternative schooling approaches must fortify young people by fostering identity formation that enables them to resist the obstacles placed in their paths and then pursue both education and aspirations that ignite their deep well of talents to achieve at high, even unparalleled levels. It's these "free" thinking, talented young people who are needed to advance and liberate Black communities locally and globally.

Readings for Transformative Education for Black Children: A Starter List

While there are many more options for developing the knowledge foundation for educating Black children, these are a few of my favorite books—all of which I believe share timeless truths.

History	**Before the Mayflower,** Lerone Bennett
	Black Athena, Martin Bernal
	Black Cargoes, Daniel Mannix
	Capitalism and Slavery, Eric Williams
	From Slavery to Freedom, John Hope Franklin
	Introduction to African Civilization, John Jackson
	They Came Before Columbus, Ivan Van Sertima
	Things Fall Apart, Chinua Achebe
	Warmth of Other Suns: The Epic Story of America's Great Migration, Isabel Wilkerson
Culture	**Autobiography of Malcolm X,** Alex Haley
	Black Boy, Richard Wright
	Bluest Eye, Toni Morrison
	I Know Why the Caged Bird Sings, Maya Angelou
	Invisible Man, Ralph Ellison
	Roll of Thunder Hear My Cry, Mildred Taylor
	The Long Dream, Richard Wright
Identity & Self Image	**Between the World and Me,** Ta-Nehisi Coates
	Black Bourgeoise, E. Franklin Frazier
	Brainwashed: Stamped from the Beginning, Tom Burrell
	Color Complex, Kathy Russell-Cole, Midge Wilson, Ronald Hall

Who Dropped the Ball on our Kids? Sondai K. Lester

Destruction of Black Civilization, Chancellor Williams

Garvey and Garveyism, Amy Jacques Garvey

Man, God and Civilization, John Jackson

Mis-education of the Negro, Carter G. Woodson

The New Jim Crow, Michelle Alexander

Outliers: The Story of Success, Malcolm Gladwell

Philosophies and Opinions of Marcus Garvey, Marcus M. Garvey

Race the History of an Idea, Thomas F. Gossett

The Souls of Black Folks, W.E.B. Dubois

Stamped from the Beginning, Ibram X. Kendi

21st **Century Skills**	**21**st **Century Skills,** Bernie Trilling and Charles Fadel
	Creating Innovators, Tony Wagner
	The Global Achievement Gap, Tony Wagner
	Third Wave, Eric Toffler

A Worksheet: 10 Things Parents Can Do
That Make a Big Difference

There are many actions and attitudes you can adopt that positively impact your children's identity formation. You can plant seeds of excellence daily and raise confident, competent Black children.

Using the worksheet below, reflect on how your parenting impacts your child's identity formation by responding to each question. Then choose what seeds (actions) you will plant to help set a foundation for excellence. **Complete one sheet for each child.**

① **Objects and Images:** Look around the house. What racially affirming objects & images are visible to your child at home?

_____

_____

_____

Action: Identify one action you can take to enhance the positive racial identity in your home.

_____

② **Language Reflection:** How would you categorize the most common type of communication you have with your child?
_____Positive & affirming
_____Mostly critical and judging
_____I use a lot of harsh language
_____ I don't talk much with my child

Action: What action can you take to improve your ability to interact meaningfully with your child?

_____

Who Dropped the Ball on our Kids? Sondai K. Lester

❸ Materials: What African-centered books, audio-visual and electronic materials do you provide for your child?

_____

_____

_____

Action: Identify two items or experiences you will add to broaden your child's exposure to positive books and other materials about his or her heritage and race.

_____

_____

❹ Strength Patterns: Name three positive characteristics possessed by your child.

_____

_____

Action: What two things can you do to reinforce and strengthen these three positive characteristics?

_____

_____

❺ Traits to Develop: What one characteristic or behavior do you need to help your child cultivate?

_____

Action: What one thing can you do to help cultivate this needed characteristic?

_____

❻ Conversations: What was the topic of the last conversation you had with your child that was *not related* to some type of misbehavior?

_____

Who Dropped the Ball on our Kids? Sondai K. Lester

Action: What is a good topic for conversation that you can use more frequently with your child (not related to misbehaving)?

_____

7 **Outside Exposure**: What types of racially positive experiences or activities do you provide for your child outside of the home?

_____
_____
_____

Action: Over the next six months, what two outside of the home experiences can you add to your child's extracurricular activities?

_____
_____

8 **School Experiences**: What educational experiences (and how frequently) does your child's school offer that teaches about their African/African American history and culture?

_____
_____
_____

Action: What else can you do to help the school enhance Black children's knowledge of their history and culture?

_____
_____
_____

⑨ Community Engagement: What type of community service activities do you and your child participate in (list those during the last 12 months)?

_____
_____
_____

Action: What one new action can you take to enhance your family's sense of service to the community?

_____

⑩ Your Expectations: When you think about your child, what are five statements that express your expectations for him or her?

_____
_____
_____
_____
_____

Action: When you look at your list, what one thing can you do to raise your expectations of your child (realizing children have amazing potential)?

_____
_____

Happy Parenting! Return to this worksheet at least quarterly to continue taking actions that help your child develop a healthy sense of self—the foundation for high achievement.

Who Dropped the Ball on our Kids? Sondai K. Lester

Author Biography

Sondai K. Lester has spent much of his life leading, teaching, researching, and writing, with education as a central theme in his commitment to social change. His experiences and leadership have ranged across the social sector: as public school and university teacher; board of education region vice chair; Atlanta Housing Commission chair; a lead minister and theologian at the Pan-African Orthodox Christian Church in Detroit and Atlanta for more than 25 years; leader of Black male, fatherhood and early childhood learning initiatives for City of Detroit Head Start; educational consultant to school leaders; and service on numerous community boards. He has taught and trained scores of ministers in liberation theology and helped transform the lives of thousands seeking racial uplift, reclamation of self-worth and a path to social change through the Christian experience.

He is a teacher, mentor, friend, and leader. He is consultant and founder of P.S.E. Institute (Planting Seeds of Excellence), which is committed to laying the foundation for excellence among generations of socially-conscious leaders and learners. He continues as a 50+ years' member of Kappa Alpha Psi.

Sondai has a Master of Arts in Teaching and underwent doctoral studies in Educational Administration. To augment his theological work, he attended seminary at Atlanta's Interdenominational Theological Center.

He is father of two adult children, Tarik and Noni, grandfather to Jide Folarin Olayinka, and Lindiwe Stovall Lester's devoted spouse.